The Expectant Father

the text of this book is printed on 100% recycled paper

About the Author

Dr. George Schaefer is Professor of Clinical Obstetrics and Gynecology at Cornell University Medical College, Attending Obstetrician and Gynecologist at The New York Lying-In Hospital, and Consultant Obstetrician and Gynecologist at Booth Memorial Medical Center. He graduated from New York University and received his M.D. degree from Cornell University Medical College.

Dr. Schaefer is the author of two textbooks, *Manual of Obstetrics* (with H. C. Williamson) and *Tuberculosis in Obstetrics and Gynecology*, and has written many articles for medical journals. He is Consultant Editor of the journal *Clinical Obstetrics and Gynecology*.

He is a Diplomate of the American Board of Obstetrics and Gynecology, a Fellow of the American College of Obstetricians and Gynecologists, a Fellow of the American College of Surgeons, and a member of the New York Obstetrical Society, the Queens Gynecological Society, and numerous other scientific organizations.

Dr. Schaefer has delivered thousands of babies in the course of his career and has therefore had the opportunity of talking with and advising many expectant fathers.

The Expectant Father

by George Schaefer, M.D.

BARNES & NOBLE BOOKS
A DIVISION OF HARPER & ROW, PUBLISHERS
New York, Evanston, San Francisco, London

This book was originally published by Simon and Schuster.

THE EXPECTANT FATHER, REVISED EDITION. Copyright © 1964 by George Schaefer and Milton L. Zisowitz. Copyright © 1972 by George Schaefer. All rights reserved. Printed in the United States of America. No part of this book may be used or reproduced in any manner without written permission except in the case of brief quotations embodied in critical articles and reviews. For information address Harper & Row, Publishers, Inc., 10 East 53rd Street, New York, N.Y. 10022. Published simultaneously in Canada by Fitzhenry & Whiteside Limited, Toronto.

First BARNES & NOBLE BOOKS edition published 1972.

LIBRARY OF CONGRESS CATALOG CARD NUMBER: 72-188794

STANDARD BOOK NUMBER: 06-463331-4

Dedicated to my wife, Shirley,
and to our children,
Jay and Michael

Contents

Foreword

In his foreword to the first edition of *The Expectant Father*, my distinguished predecessor, Professor R. Gordon Douglas, stressed the role of the father, not only in the upbringing and education of his children, but also in support of his wife during pregnancy and, in many instances, during delivery. Dr. Douglas initiated the parent education program at The New York Hospital almost twenty years ago, a program which has permitted countless couples to share the task of preparing themselves for parenthood. It allows the father to be present in the labor and delivery rooms and to lend support to his wife while sharing the unique experience of the birth of their baby.

At a time when family planning is the word of the day, it is worthwhile to remember that family planning is not synonymous with contraception. It is a biological instinct to reproduce, as essential for survival of the human race as breathing is for each human individual. But, in the human, one can regard reproduction as a by-product of sexual life, certainly not as its sole purpose. We are concerned today with the quality of life, and while we do not want to suppress the biological urge to reproduce, we want to give our offspring a life of the highest quality.

In the complex life of the modern, urbanized civilization, this requires planning. This book provides a fund of information for a prospective father, and the success of the first edition amply documents that it fills a need.

Every day it seems to become more difficult to be a good father.

Some of those who recently have been faced with the generation gap may well, in thinking back, consider the concern and worries during the nine months before the birth of the first baby as a heavenly time. Indeed, those nine months can be heavenly when all goes well and both prospective parents are prepared for the task before them. With this book, which Dr. Schaefer has brought up to date with extensive revisions and the addition of new information, any man can look forward to fatherhood with a sense of being well prepared, at least for the first part of it.

The additions include a section on premature labor, a section on fetology and fetal monitoring during pregnancy and labor, and a chapter on hereditary disorders and genetic counseling. Also included are discussions of abortion and contraception, natural childbirth and the Lamaze method of relaxation, and the pros and cons of breast feeding.

Dr. George Schaefer, Professor of Clinical Obstetrics and Gynecology, Cornell University Medical College, has been associated with The New York Hospital–Cornell Medical Center for many years. With long experience from the hospital, his private practice, and his own family, he has much to offer the prospective father.

As predicted by Dr. Douglas, *The Expectant Father* immediately took its place beside the many excellent books for expectant mothers. The book is truly an aid to expectant fathers in understanding the important role of fatherhood and will help them play that role successfully, with great satisfaction.

FRITZ F. FUCHS, M.D.

Preface

In the eight years since the first edition of *The Expectant Father*, many new and exciting advances have taken place in obstetrics, and in the next decade we anticipate even further progress. I started this revision simply to update the material but finished the task with nine new chapters and revisions in many of the remaining ones.

My task was made more difficult by the death, several years ago, of my former co-author, Milton L. Zisowitz, author of the chapter "Toys for the Baby, Not for You" and the appendix "Names, Names, Names." Almost all of what he wrote eight years ago is still true today; only minimal updating was necessary, a fact I know would have pleased him.

By new and sophisticated techniques, the health and development of the fetus *in utero* can be followed throughout pregnancy. Advances in the diagnosis and prevention of Rh disease and German measles are examples of conditions that were once a serious threat to the normal development of the fetus which can now be controlled and hopefully eradicated in the future. A great deal more is now known about the effect of drugs on the unborn infant, and all of the newer information about congenital anomalies is discussed in greater detail.

The chapter "Education for Parenthood" has been expanded to include psychoprophylaxis, a method of preparation for parenthood which has become increasingly popular in the past five years. In conjunction with the newer knowledge in fetal medicine, more accurate methods of assessing the condition of the fetus in labor have been developed and they are discussed in this edition.

I should like to express my appreciation to Dr. Fritz Fuchs, Professor of Obstetrics and Gynecology at Cornell University Medical College and Obstetrician and Gynecologist-in-Chief of The New York Hospital, who read the entire manuscript, made valuable suggestions, and wrote the foreword to this edition.

I am most grateful to Dr. John T. Queenan for the suggestions included in the chapter on Rh disease, and to Dr. Joe L. Simpson, a specialist in medical genetics, for his discussion of genes and chromosomes. Dr. Abraham Weinberg aided with the material on hypnosis in obstetrics.

Mrs. Elizabeth Bing, who was instrumental in popularizing psychoprophylaxis in obstetrics in the United States, and the nurses who teach the course at The New York Lying-In Hospital —Miss Dorothy Metzger, Mrs. Fritzi Kallop, Mrs. Ruth Merkatz, and Miss Polly Seitz—offered suggestions on this subject when I attended their classes. Mrs. Marretjé Buhrer, who gives the course at Booth Memorial Medical Center, also offered her valuable assistance.

I wish to express my appreciation to my former secretary, Mrs. Anita Atkinson, who came out of retirement to decipher my handwritten hieroglyphics, retype this manuscript, and yet maintain sufficient sanity to return to her family. To Mrs. Marie Wolf go special thanks for the hours she spent pasting up and organizing the new and old.

My wife Shirley deserves gratitude and affection not only for her encouragement and advice but also for her understanding when I lost social contact by withdrawing to my office to work on this revision.

The Expectant Father

CHAPTER 1

The Premarital Examination for Men

How many men think of having a premarital examination? I don't mean a blood test and a congratulatory handshake, but a complete physical examination including examination of the genital organs, a reproductive history, and a frank discussion with the physician. How many men ask their physician's advice concerning sexual intercourse, marital counseling, the honeymoon, and the first months of marriage?

The majority of prospective bridegrooms have some foundation for initiating the mechanical aspects of coitus, but some require private counseling. All should clearly understand the slowness of the female in being sexually aroused, and that the husband should assist her in making the adjustment, with tenderness, understanding, and delicacy.

It comes as a surprise to many young couples that physical enjoyment of sex is a learned technique. Without ever having been confronted with this reality, each of the partners may have assumed that when the proper time came, all would be revealed to them. Not so!

The couple should be told that immediate, spontaneous exaltation and satisfaction are not always possible from the marriage night onward. Instead, there usually develops an increasing ability for each to enjoy the other's body. It may take weeks, months, or even years before total satisfaction is possible. Most important, they should discuss with each other what is pleasurable and what

1

is not. Don't ask the boys in the office what happens with their wives, and don't rely on your premarital experience with other women!

One of the major problems of the bridegroom is premature ejaculation, which frequently results from lack of confidence and control. Time, patience, and understanding of both marital partners allows improved coordination and control and eliminates premature ejaculation.

It is important for adequate premarital counseling that both partners be present. What is said in the interview will depend on the problems of the particular couple, but there are a few points of advice that are important.

First, the bride and groom must understand that one should not make love by mechanical plan, as one uses the manual of arms in a military drill. Following the various steps indicated in a marriage manual is not the prerequisite of successful coitus. Sexual intercourse is a beautiful and mature expression of love which should be conveyed according to the personalities of the two individuals; it should be communicated with warmth, understanding, tenderness, and originality. It is by no means the most important aspect of marriage, but it is a relationship which affirms the physical as well as the emotional side.

Second, enjoyment of the sex act is not always natural, instinctive, or guaranteed. Only in the human being is the sex act separated from the primary function of reproduction. In humans, sex for producing children is secondary to sex for pleasure. The confusion and interplay of these two motives, procreation and pleasure, in human beings would seem to be basic causes for many of our problems.

Third, the female responds more slowly to sexual stimulation than does the male. During certain phases of the monthly cycle, some females seem to be more receptive than at other times. In general, however, the female requires a period of preliminary sexual foreplay in order to ready her.

Fourth, the clitoris is the main erotic trigger for the woman. Its manipulation, plus vulvar, thigh, breast, and lip stimulation are all important to the foreplay period. The eager husband sometimes does not understand this. Tactile sensation is not enough, however. Creating a mood for loving is most important, and failure to do this can nullify techniques of stimulation. It is hard for a wife to quarrel with her husband and then respond to him sexually.

Fifth, the vagina is essentially a canal with very little sensation. It is an excellent structure for delivering a baby, but when used in the sexual function, the vagina communicates very little sensation other than deep pressure. More sensation may develop as the marriage goes on. Orgasm takes place as a result of sensation originating in the clitoris.

Some discussion of family planning should take place before marriage. The various techniques of contraception should be known to the prospective groom as well as to the bride. These are discussed in detail in Chapter 20.

CHAPTER 2

First Visit to the Doctor

Nowadays, most wives do not blushingly confess to their husbands that they are expecting "a blessed event," nor do they shyly hint a baby is on the way by such coy devices as "knitting little things." They usually announce their pregnancy frankly and often proudly. Indeed, most husbands and wives now plan together for their future family. Husbands often receive the big news with little surprise and with a good deal of enthusiasm. They are eager to help their wives through a satisfying experience, and they look forward to playing a full and active role in bringing up the baby. If you are one of these happy expectant fathers, you can start well by insisting that your wife obtain prenatal care early in her pregnancy, by helping to select a doctor, and by going along on her first visit to his office.

Prenatal care, the regular and careful supervision of the pregnant woman, is responsible for tremendous improvement in the safety and welfare of both mothers and babies and has also prevented many miscarriages, which, though not too common, are most likely to occur during the first three months of pregnancy. Your wife should see a doctor as soon as she suspects that she is pregnant—one or two weeks after the first missed menstrual period— and certainly after the second missed period. To delay because "Mother never went to a doctor until she bulged," or because "I feel perfectly well and haven't a single complaint in the world" is unwise and could be harmful.

Choosing Your Doctor

Once you've decided to seek medical advice, the next question is whether to go to an obstetrician, who has been specially trained to meet any emergency, to your family doctor, whom you know as a friend and confidant, or to a clinic, if one is available. Some factors that may influence your final decision are the local hospital and medical facilities, any previous illnesses your wife may have had, financial considerations, and the advice and opinions of friends and relatives. If you are new in the community or don't want to rely on personal recommendations, the county medical society of the local voluntary hospital will provide a list of obstetricians and general practitioners. The medical society can also tell you where to inquire about clinic accommodations if you prefer this type of care.

No matter who the doctor is, he'll probably want to see you and your wife together, preferably at the first visit. He will ask you to remain in the waiting room while he takes your wife's complete medical history and gives her a careful physical examination. Then he'll speak to you both and give verbal as well as written instructions, which he may modify as pregnancy progresses. Among the things he will discuss with you are diet, vitamins and minerals, hygiene, intercourse, travel, exercise, selection of a hospital, and financial arrangements.

Take Nothing for Granted

Now is the time to ask questions. If in your excitement you forget some, or if additional questions come up later, jot them down and have your wife get the answers at another visit. Take few things for granted, and don't be afraid of appearing naïve.

Watch Your Own Weight

Diet and weight control are always important, but are especially so during pregnancy. While the legend about "eating for two" has long been discredited, your wife should eat a well-balanced diet, which her doctor will discuss with her. If she gains a normal amount of weight—and her doctor will tell her what that should be, depending on her height and build—she will be more comfortable throughout pregnancy, have an easier labor and delivery, bear a healthier baby, and look better afterward. If she grows too heavy, she runs an added risk of certain hazards, among the most serious of which is toxemia, a complication of pregnancy associated with high blood pressure, swelling of the hands and feet, and albumin in the urine. Added weight also places an abnormal burden on the heart, causes shortness of breath, discomfort, clumsiness, and may increase the danger of falling. But what may convince your wife more than any medical reason is that if she becomes overweight during pregnancy, she may find it difficult to reduce afterward, and thus might remain fat. You can help by eating sensibly in her presence and by resisting the temptation to shower her with boxes of candy and other fattening treats. Incidentally, you can improve your own physical condition by taking this opportunity to watch your diet as well as hers.

Exercise without Exertion

Both you and your wife should clearly understand her doctor's instructions about exercise, travel, automobile driving, employment, and other activities. One outdoor man, always unhappy about the nonathletic habits of his wife, interpreted permission to swim during pregnancy as an order to take up the sport. When the doctor heard about this, he explained to the husband that it was not wise for a pregnant woman to engage in any unaccustomed physical activity, although it was equally bad for her to avoid all exercise. He suggested that the couple might try to explore the pleasures of walking.

As a rule, your wife will be told to continue her ordinary activities throughout pregnancy, but to get more than the usual amount of rest and to avoid becoming overtired. Whether or not she should continue to work, and for how long, depends upon such factors as the type of job, the distance traveled and mode of transportation, the household chores that must be performed after she comes home, and her attitude toward employment. Usually, working at a relatively sedentary occupation is permitted and may be continued as long as it does not interfere with comfort. Often an enjoyable job makes a pregnancy easier because it makes a woman feel useful, keeps her mentally and physically occupied, and helps make the time pass more quickly.

Don't Be Shy

Don't be too shy to ask the doctor about intercourse during pregnancy. An oversolicitous husband moved his bed to the living room as soon as he found out that his wife was pregnant. His mother had suffered a series of miscarriages, and he mistakenly assumed that these had been the result of sexual relations. His wife finally mustered enough courage to mention the matter to her doctor, who telephoned the husband and assured him that celibacy was neither necessary nor desirable in this particular case. Unless there are specific medical contraindications—and your wife's physician is the only one qualified to judge in this matter—you and your wife may continue to enjoy sexual relations up to the eighth month at least. Your doctor may suggest you abstain during the first three months on those days when she would ordinarily be having her menstrual period (this is the time when miscarriages most frequently occur).

This is also the time to discuss hospitals and fees with the doctor. If he is connected with more than one institution, you will want to know about the location and facilities of each before making a final choice. You will want to know about private and semiprivate accommodations, rooming-in plans, and other matters. You will certainly want to know what the baby is going to cost you. Be frank, and the doctor will be equally frank with you.

Celebrate Good News

When you and your wife leave the doctor's office after the first visit, celebrate! Take her to a special place for lunch, for cocktails or for dinner—the diet can wait! Show her that you are as happy as she is about your mutual good fortune. Let her know that this moment is just as important and exciting to you as it is to her. The next nine months will allow for a closeness and a happiness in your life together that you have not yet experienced. Both of you are going to have a baby!

CHAPTER 3

A New Life Begins

The nine wonderful—and sometimes difficult—months of your wife's pregnancy are a miraculous prelude to the equally miraculous climax of birth. Contrary to superstitions still current, nothing that happens to a normal pregnant woman can affect the child's character, personality, or talents. Of course, her health, nutritional state, and the presence or absence of certain diseases do play a role in the development of the baby, and your doctor will advise you on these matters.

The union of the sperm cell from your body with the egg cell in hers determines, precisely at that moment, not only your child's sex and the color of its hair and eyes, but also many of the major aspects of its physical and psychological makeup. And there is nothing that either of you can do to change this.

A Life Begins

Having joined in the Fallopian tube,* the two sex cells, now united into what is called a fertilized egg, journey downward toward the uterus for the next three or four days, all the while dividing and subdividing into more cells. When the structure reaches the uterus, it is no longer a solid mass but a hollow sphere. By the fifth day it has grown into about sixty cells and is floating around the uterine cavity seeking and finally finding a place of attachment within a day or two. It then fastens itself to the uterine

* For the meaning of medical terms used in this book, see Appendix 2, "Doctors' Language," beginning on page 147.

wall, which has undergone appropriate physical changes to receive it. Thereafter, following some further development, it will receive all of its oxygen and nutrition from the mother's bloodstream.

An amazing process of growth and differentiation now begins, whereby all the tissues, structures, organs, and organ systems of a human body are developed. The science of genetics makes it possible to explain some of the complex biochemical processes by which a multitude of different structures, with myriad possibilities for individual variation, are formed from a single fertilized egg; but complete understanding of this mystery must await further research. In any event, you have very little to worry about, because the chances are that the baby will bear some physical and psychological resemblance to you and your wife, that it will be healthy and perfectly formed, and that, except in those rare instances where there is a familial defect, it will be completely normal. Most often, even hereditary flaws do not affect every generation. Once in a while a parent is disappointed if a minor flaw does not appear in the baby. One obstetrician tells of the time he delivered a girl who had webbed toes. As he was thinking of some way to break this news gently to the mother, she suddenly asked him what her daughter's feet looked like. When he reluctantly told her the truth, she heaved a sigh of relief, kicking her own feet out from under the covers with some pride. All the girls in her family had webbed toes, and they considered this a mark of distinction.

The Embryo Grows

By the end of about the first month, the embryo is approximately one-quarter of an inch long. It already has a backbone, a head, the rudiments of a heart, a circulatory system, a gastrointestinal tract, arms, legs, and—as evidence of the true genealogy of the species—a tail. Toward the end of the second month the embryo has begun to take on human form, and from now until birth it is called a fetus. It has a face, arms, legs, fingers, toes, elbows, and knees. The sex organs have begun to appear, but it is difficult to distinguish a girl from a boy. The tail has now reached its maximum size and hereafter will begin to shrink until it is evident only as the coccyx of the spine. Your baby is now about one inch long and weighs approximately one-thirtieth of an ounce.

One month later, the fetus has tripled in length and weighs a full ounce. Fingernails, toenails, and baby teeth have started to appear. Furthermore, a crude kidney now secretes small amounts of urine into a bladder that probably empties into the amniotic fluid and thence out of the mother's body through her kidneys.

Movements Begin

At the end of the fourth month, the fetus, now almost four ounces and six and one-half inches long, grows a layer of down (called lanugo) all over its body and a few true hairs on its scalp. For the first time, the mother will feel some movement, which will become more marked by the end of the fifth month when the fetus is about ten inches long, weighs approximately eight ounces, and has a heartbeat so strong that the doctor can hear it through his stethoscope. Sometimes the fetus will move so vigorously at this stage that the mother, although pleasantly excited, will be slightly uncomfortable. She may even be embarrassed, for, as pregnancy progresses, these movements become visible. One young couple was in a bus on the way to the movies when the husband noticed that his wife's dress was making funny little movements. He then realized, "Maybe baby is enjoying the ride too!"

Most of these movements, big and small, that a woman feels from the fifth month onward are due to the fetus exercising. It rolls and somersaults easily because it is weightless and buoyant in the bag of waters, the amniotic fluid. (The fetus is not too different from astronauts walking in space, attached by what they called an umbilical cord to the mother ship.) These exercises are necessary for the fetus to develop muscles, but naturally some movements are just simple efforts to get more comfortable.

The Fetus Is Listening Too

Recently, doctors have learned that the fetus moves in response to sounds it actually hears. After the twenty-fourth week it even hears the mother's heart and intestinal gurgles. Not only does the fetus listen, but it also produces sounds and apparently tries to imitate others.

Fetal hearing was tested and proved when a buzzer was placed against the mother's abdomen as close as possible to the fetal ear. The object was to startle the fetus so that it would "jump" and the heart beat faster. Such responses occurred and were recorded on a phonocardiograph by a team of Swedish investigators including an obstetrician, an ear specialist, and an engineer.

In several instances, and as no surprise to them, they detected fetal hearing defects and subsequently proved that they were present at birth. They predict that one day prenatal and postnatal hearing tests will be routine procedures, especially for high-risk babies. This is exciting since the earlier a hearing defect is discovered, the more can be done to correct the handicap.

Yes, The Fetus Can Swallow

By the end of the third month the fetus can swallow; this is an early important step in learning to eat. It has been estimated that it can consume up to 20 ml of fluid per hour or about a pint (one-half liter) per day. When the doctor has precise knowledge of amniotic fluid volume as well as the rate of fetal consumption of fluid, it is anticipated that he will be able to administer medication to the fetus by injecting it directly into the amniotic cavity. This will be welcomed as another positive step in medicine!

Premature Birth

During the last few months the fetus grows rapidly, and all of its structures begin to take definite form. At the end of the sixth month, it is twelve inches long and weighs a pound and a half. At the end of the seventh month, it has grown an additional three inches and gained a pound. Even if it is born now, it has a fair chance of survival, especially with the modern methods of caring for premature babies. And, contrary to another superstition, its chances of living are better by far at the end of the eighth month when it is about sixteen and a half inches long and weighs approximately four pounds.

Premature Labor

Many of us have used the expression "born too soon" to refer to a person who would have enjoyed living in a later century or whose life's work might have had a greater impact on the world had he been born later. For the fetus, "born too soon" has far greater significance. It may mean its very life. Premature labor or delivery before the thirty-sixth week of gestation is still one of the important problems in obstetrics.

Premature infants are those weighing less than five and one-half pounds or born at least four weeks before the expected date. They comprise about 10 percent of all live births and have a far higher mortality rate than full-term infants. Almost 15 percent die during the first week of life. The mature infant has a mortality rate of less than one-half percent.

While the causes of prematurity are exceedingly variable, including such predisposing factors as socioeconomic, nutritional, medical, and psychosomatic, the various ministrations to prevent prematurity have not been successful. The use of hormones to stop uterine contractions has failed. New drugs are being tested and some demonstrate ability to inhibit uterine contraction and perhaps prolong gestation; however, such drugs are still in the experimental stage.

A new procedure, the intravenous injection of alcohol, has been successfully used at The New York Lying-In Hospital for the past five years. It has been possible to arrest premature labor in two out of three patients, if the membranes have not yet ruptured. Apparently alcohol works by blocking the release of those hormones which initiate uterine contractions and maintain labor. The doses of alcohol necessary to arrest premature labor have no harmful effect on the fetus and aside from making mother a little drunk, have no deleterious effect on her. In some instances, when intravenous alcohol was not readily available, the mother took alcohol by mouth and achieved the same effect on the impending labor.

Full Term

Over the next few weeks, the fetus, now a mature infant for all practical purposes, gains about half a pound each week and makes a remarkable improvement in appearance. By the end of this period, when full term has been reached, the baby weighs an average of seven pounds if it is a girl, seven and a half if it is a boy, and is about twenty inches long. The weight and length of a baby are basically determined by the weight and height of the parents. Contrary to mistaken notions, a woman who gains a lot of weight during pregnancy will not necessarily have a heavy baby. Indeed, this excessive weight gain may be associated with toxemia, a condition that could result in a small baby. By the time it reaches term, the baby's delicate skin is covered with a cheese-like protective coating, the fingernails are firm, and many infants have a fairly full head of hair. At any time now, it is ready to leave the protection of the womb and emerge into the outside world.

All Babies Are Beautiful

If you are like most brand-new fathers, you'll be disappointed, perhaps even shocked, when you see your baby soon after birth. The head will seem large compared to the rest of the body, and may be misshapen owing to the pressure it sustained in its passage through the birth canal. Don't worry. It will come back to shape within a few days. The chest will be narrow and the abdomen large. The pink or red skin is likely to be wrinkled. The head may be covered with a mass of hair, usually dark, but this soon falls out, leaving the baby quite bald until the new crop grows in. The fingernails, which have developed fully during prenatal life, are often so long that they must be cut to keep the baby from scratching himself. Hearing is well developed, and the baby is sensitive to noises. He can tell light from dark, but can see little else for the first few days. The eyes frequently cross because the muscles controlling them are not yet fully developed. In a few days, coordination of muscles and nerves is achieved and the baby begins to see.

No matter how long or hard he cries, there will be no tears, for the glands which make them will not begin to work for several weeks. The stump of the umbilical cord will be protruding from the abdomen, but in about a week it will dry up and fall off.

CHAPTER 4

What You Can Expect

Even before your baby is born, a great deal of factual information can be determined to safeguard its survival. A new branch of medicine which is concerned with the fetus and its environment and whose practitioners are called fetologists, is becoming one of the most promising and fascinating fields in modern medicine. Some of the methods they use to study the condition of the fetus and to render a prenatal diagnosis are most ingenious.

Hormone Determination in Mothers

There is a correlation between the excretion of a specific hormone in maternal urine and the status of the fetoplacental environment. This hormone is called estriol. Frequent serial determinations of this hormone obtained from the mother's urine or blood may enable the doctor to detect any early danger to the fetus. Such a test is particularly useful in what doctors commonly refer to as high-risk pregnancies, those complicated by toxemia and diabetes. The early recognition of danger permits the doctor to intervene promptly to improve fetal survival, perhaps even by removing it from its hostile environment. This hormone test can also be of value in conjunction with other clinical and laboratory procedures such as amniocentesis and amnioscopy.

Amniocentesis

By needle puncture through the abdominal skin, muscle, and uterine wall of the mother, the doctor withdraws fluid and cells from the bag of waters surrounding the fetus. The procedure was first used many years ago to withdraw this same fluid when it was present in an excess amount, a condition referred to as hydramnios.

In amniocentesis, the amniotic fluid withdrawn is examined chemically, cytologically, and spectrophotometrically. As we shall see in Chapters 5 and 6, this medical procedure has many valuable indications, its most important being in cases of Rh immunization for which repeated withdrawal of amniotic fluid may begin in the twenty-sixth to twenty-eighth week of pregnancy. It has been used in conjunction with amniography, an X-ray technique, to determine fetal anomalies. Moreover, amniocentesis is also useful in determining postmaturity, in determining the sex of the fetus, and in obtaining cells for culture to determine certain genetic anomalies such as mongolism. Occasionally, it is used to manage better maternal diabetes and toxemia of pregnancy.

The earliest use of amniotic fluid examination to identify and prevent sex-linked hereditary disorders such as hemophilia or muscular dystrophy (which are described in the next chapter) was in 1960 by Dr. Pavl Riis and Dr. Fritz Fuchs. Although unable to diagnose the disease directly, they could determine the sex of the fetus, and since, with rare exceptions, only the male inherits the disease, selective preventive measures could be taken. Doctors Riis and Fuchs were also the first to use therapeutic abortion in carriers of hemophilia.

Then in 1961 Dr. Fuchs and Dr. John Philip recommended the use of amniocentesis as a method to obtain human amniotic fluid cells for culture to diagnose chromosomal abnormalities. In 1966 this method was first used to identify mothers who had a high risk of giving birth to children with chromosomal abnormalities. These tests are now available to genetic counselors who advise parents whether to continue a pregnancy or have it interrupted therapeutically.

The intrauterine diagnosis of a hereditary disease was recently made by a group of physicians at Brooklyn's Kingsbrook Jewish

Medical Center by means of amniocentesis and biochemical analysis of the amniotic fluid. The woman was in her second pregnancy. Her first had been a tragedy. She had seen her apparently healthy infant wither and die, a victim of the hereditary metabolic disorder called Tay-Sachs disease. Would this same thing happen again?

To allay, or confirm, her fears, doctors performed amniocentesis in the middle of her pregnancy. Analysis of the fluid obtained showed it to be lacking an enzyme, hexosaminase component A. The absence of this enzyme is now known to cause Tay-Sachs disease and related disorders. Finding the vital enzyme absent, they performed a therapeutic abortion and were able to confirm their diagnosis upon examination of the aborted fetus.

Sonar (Ultrasonic Echo Sounding)

The term "sonar" stands for "sound navigation and ranging," an acknowledgment of its naval derivation. Its use in obstetrics was introduced by Professor Ian Donald of Scotland. Sonar employs sound waves of frequencies far above the range of human hearing, exceeding 20,000 cycles per second. At these frequencies, sound, like light, can be propagated as a beam under accurate directional control. Diagnostic ultrasonic techniques utilize the reflected sound wave. Reflection occurs when the sound meets a material of different specific impedance, the product of the density of the material and the velocity of sound in that material. For scanning, pulsed ultrasound is used. The sound is generated and echoes are received by a ceramic crystal mounted on a probe. Compound B-scanning is the most successful method of diagnostic scanning. The echo is represented as a dot corresponding to the position of the echo. The signals are recorded from the oscilloscope screen using a Polaroid camera. Diagnostic sonar involves very low energies and has no harmful effects on the fetus, and, unlike X-rays, does not employ ionizing radiation. The picture obtained by sonar with a B-scan is from echo signals and is two-dimensional. Repeated tests are essential for accurate and reliable monitoring with sonar. This technique has been used to determine whether an early pregnancy exists, the size of the fetal head, the presence of twins, the position of the placenta, and certain physical complications. Dr. Donald states the most fascinating aspect of sonar is to observe the growth of a very early pregnancy, especially in cases of previous recurrent unsuccessful pregnancies.

Amniography

This is the injection of a radio-opaque medium which disperses uniformly throughout the amniotic fluid and enables the soft tissue of the fetus to become visible on X-ray. Before the dye is injected, a small amount of amniotic fluid is withdrawn. The primary purpose of amniography is to detect congenital anomalies which are not visible on the ordinary X-ray. When the anomalies are not correctable, termination of the pregnancy by abortion may be considered as soon as this is safe for the mother.

Amnioscopy

Another useful procedure for studying the fetus is amnioscopy. This is the visualization of the color of the amniotic fluid through the intact membranes. It is performed by inserting a hollow, conical tube equipped with a strong light source through a partially dilated cervix. The procedure is particularly useful in high-risk pregnancies, those complicated by postmaturity, diabetes, and toxemia near term. If the amniotic fluid is colored, this observation in conjunction with other clinical findings may be used as a helpful aid in management. It is a harmless procedure that does not require hospitalization and can be repeated as often as is necessary.

Determination of Age of Fetus

At times it is important to determine the exact age of the fetus in order to terminate a pregnancy in such conditions as diabetes, Rh disease, toxemia, or in prolonged pregnancy where longer gestation might be harmful to the fetus. It is also necessary for the doctor to know the exact age of the fetus before performing a repeat Caesarean section so that this procedure is not done too early resulting in delivery of a premature infant. No method heretofore available was capable of providing the doctor with exact information.

In the past few years several new tests have been tried. One is examination of the fetal cells in the amniotic fluid for lipid substances or fat. This test measures the percentage of orange-stained cells after staining with a Nile blue sulphate. A sharp rise in these cells is found after the thirty-eighth week of gestation and is thought to be due to the functional maturity of the superficial cells of the skin or of the sebaceous glands of the fetus. This test, in addition to the total number of cells per cubic millimeter in the amniotic fluid, and a Papanicolaou cell count for cornified and precornified cells, gives a fairly accurate determination of fetal age and reduces the frequency of early induction of labor resulting in prematurity and its complications.

The determination of the concentration of creatinine in the amniotic fluid is another method for assessing fetal maturity. When the creatinine is above a certain level the fetal age is thirty-six weeks or more. This latter test is perhaps the most accurate single test for estimating fetal maturity.

Boy or Girl?

A historical view of past antenatal sex determination collected by Dr. Lars Cederqvist and Dr. Fuchs in 1970 pointed out many past unsuccessful and bizarre attempts to predict the sex of the unborn child. In old Egyptian medical records, circa 1350 B.C., the sex of the unborn child was determined by the color of the mother's face. A pregnant woman whose face had a greenish hue could be sure of giving birth to a boy. At the time of Hippocrates, it was taught that if the expectant mother had a good color she was carrying a male, whereas if her color was poor she would give birth to a girl.

The thoughts and dreams of the woman during gestation also were thought to be significant in determining sex. During the tenth century the Japanese believed that women desiring boys should think of male activities such as hunting. In India, any dreams about men's food indicated the pregnant woman was carrying a boy, while in Russia, dreams of knives and clubs were associated with boys, while dreams of parties signified a girl.

Right-sided signs were also thought to indicate a male fetus. The right side of the body was always considered the stronger and more valuable side and the male the stronger and superior sex. In the sixth century it was taught that the right breast would be larger and secrete milk earlier if a male were expected. Other signs associated with a male were: the woman's right eye would be brighter and more sparkling with a larger pupil, and the right nostril would have a greater tendency to bleed. It was also believed that the right ovary produced male offspring and the left ovary females. Another opinion that one still hears is that the right and left ovary alternate each month in discharging ova, and that the male-determining ova always come from the right ovary and the female-determining ova from the left ovary.

Another and still prevalent belief, based on a study of 100 cases in 1859, is that fetal sex can be predicted from fetal heart rate during the last three months of pregnancy. A slow rate of 124 per minute or less is said to be a boy, while a more rapid rate of 144 or more per minute indicates a girl. I know of no obstetrician who would attempt to predict sex on the basis of the fetal heart rate.

It is now possible to determine the sex of your unborn child by one of several methods. The most accurate is amniocentesis, specifically examining the cells contained in the fluid for presence or absence of sex chromatin. The presence of sex chromatin or Barr bodies in the cells implies a female fetus. Its absence indicates a male. While amniocentesis is a simple procedure when performed after the twenty-fourth week of pregnancy, it is never completely innocuous and when attempted too early in pregnancy may give rise to complications. Therefore, it should not be done solely to satisfy curiosity about the sex of an unborn child. There isn't anything you can do to change it anyway!

Recently several doctors at the San Francisco Medical Center reported a method for prenatal sex determination of male fetuses by examining the mother's blood. After the fourteenth week of pregnancy certain blood cells (lymphocytes) of the fetus pass into the mother's circulation. The sex chromosome complement of these cells was identified as XY indicating a male fetus. Sex predictability of a female fetus was less reliable and more complicated by this test than by the one described above.

Two to Grow on

Don't worry about twins either. Fraternal twins are determined by heredity, identical twins by chance and there are some differences among races. Negroes have the best chance for twins, whites slightly less and Orientals the least of all. If your wife is under twenty, her chances of twinning are 1 in 167. As she grows older, they increase, reaching a peak at the age of thirty-five or forty, when they are 1 in 74. If, however, she is having her seventh pregnancy at that age, the chances are 1 in 45 that you will be the father of twins. After forty-five, the chances of bearing twins are about the same as they were at twenty. Of course, your family tree is important in respect to fraternal twins. If such twins have appeared on either side, the chances are increased; if both families boast of twins, you are likely to carry on the tradition sooner or later.

Your Child Is Unique

In addition to the genes for sex, there are other genes in your sperm cell and in your wife's egg cell that determine the characteristics of your child. Many couples are unclear about the nature and function of these genes, and therefore equally unclear about what they can expect of their children. Every child is an individual, different in some respect from every other child born in the past or who may be born in the future. (The only exception to this rule arises in the case of identical twins, who share certain genetic characteristics.) Nor will the child necessarily reflect the characteristics or personalities of his parents. The infant may look and behave more like a grandparent or some other more distant blood relative. Since there is nothing you and your wife can do about this genetic structure, you might as well be prepared to accept your baby as is. Most children thrive if you love them for what they are, if you don't try to impose your personality and will on them, and if you guide them to develop naturally and happily.

After asking about his baby's sex, a new father is most likely to ask about weight. Here, too, there are many variations depending upon the build of the parents, the health of the mother during pregnancy, whether the child is a first baby, and many other factors. Most babies achieve the normal weight and height of a twenty-one-year-old by the time they become twenty-one.

CHAPTER 5

More about Genes
and Chromosomes

An expectant father may think all babies look alike, but when his baby is born, he will immediately notice how it differs from all other infants. Some differences such as skin or hair color are obvious; other differences such as blood type are detected only by special tests. The precise differences are controlled by hereditary units called genes which number in the thousands for each person. Like it or not, your child will look like you because genes are transmitted from parent to child. One-half of the infant's genes are derived from the mother, one-half from the father, and the combination is never precisely the same in siblings unless they are identical twins.

Genes are located in a definite position in a structure called a chromosome, pairs of which are present within the nucleus of every cell in the body. Every living cell of each species has a characteristic number of paired chromosomes; the normal number in man is twenty-three pairs. Twenty-two of these structurally identical pairs are called autosomes. The remaining pair, known as the sex chromosomes (XX or XY), determines, in addition to other characteristics, the sex of an individual. In the female, the pair is composed of two identical X chromosomes. In the male a dissimilar pair is composed of one X and one Y chromosome.

You might suppose that since the egg and sperm cell nuclei meet at fertilization, the number of chromosomes would double from generation to generation. But this does not happen because before fertilization a particular kind of division reduces the number of the sex chromosomes and the autosomes by one-half. Only when the egg cell and the sperm cell each have twenty-three chromosomes are these sex cells mature and capable of undergoing fertilization. When an egg cell is fertilized by a sperm containing an X chromosome, a female embryo will result. If the ovum is fertilized by a sperm containing a Y chromosome, a male will result. So it is the father who determines the sex of the infant and the mother has little if anything to do with it!

Once the egg and the sperm unite, a fertilized cell with forty-six chromosomes is produced, twenty-three of which came from the mother and twenty-three from the father. This one cell then divides in two with division accomplished in such a way that the two daughter cells each have forty-six chromosomes, too. The daughter cells contain the same genetic information contained in the parent cell. This process of division goes on throughout embryonic (fetal) development and throughout adult life as well. The chances are that this development will be normal.

But one of the first questions a new mother asks after giving birth is whether her baby is normal. In most cases the doctor can reassure her that she has a healthy infant. Doctors notice that the new father is just as apprehensive. Usually these parental fears about conceiving an abnormal child, although natural, are needless. Remember that the process by which a fetus develops is quite complex, and it is not surprising that occasionally the process is not completed perfectly. An infant may then be born with one or more birth defects, but it is, indeed, a rather small percentage of parents who have children with congenital defects. Yet when confronted with this situation they want to know why it happened. Whose fault was it? Can the baby be cured? Will it happen again?

During the past few years, advances in knowledge about causes of birth defects have made it possible for the genetic counselor, a new kind of medical specialist, to predict the likelihood of transmitting certain defects and diseases. Most often, counselors are consulted by a couple who have had a child born with a congenital defect, or by parents of a child who later develops an inherited metabolic disease.

A genetic counselor cannot make predictions with absolute certainty. What he can do after he has completed his investigation is to give parents a firm idea of their chances of having a normal child or of having a child with the inherited condition in question. For example, he can say that there is one chance in two in one case, or less than one in fifty in another case, of a recurrence of a particular congenital defect that occurred in the first-born child. Occasionally, this specialist can do more than predict the probability of a defect. In a case such as phenylketonuria (PKU), a condition due to a dietary disorder, he can suggest treatment to forestall the effects of this condition. By testing the newborn for PKU, dietary treatment can be instituted early enough to prevent severe mental retardation which otherwise would develop in babies born with this disorder.

Some birth defects may result predominantly from an environmental cause. Examples are the pregnant woman who acquires German measles (rubella), or the pregnant woman who takes a drug such as thalidomide, a dangerous compound now withdrawn from the market. If an infant develops defects or anomalies as a result of such an environmental cause, the same defect is not likely to recur in subsequent pregnancies. But when the birth defect results from genetic errors, these may sometimes recur.

Problems with Chromosomes

Birth defects can result from too many or too few chromosomes, or from fusion or merely rearrangement resulting in addition to or deletion from only part of a chromosome. Because each of these structures contains many genes, abnormalities in many body systems can occur when there are errors in chromosome number. Mongolism, for example, is a genetic disorder caused by one too many of a particular chromosome. Very often chromosomal abnormalities result not in birth defects but in miscarriage. Nevertheless, if a couple has had one infant with a numerical chromosomal problem, it is unlikely that the problem will recur in subsequent children.

In one rare and special instance called "translocation," however, a recurrence of chromosomal anomalies (birth defects) is more likely. Translocation is a situation in which parts or all of two chromosomes have become joined together, yet it may or may not manifest itself as a birth defect. Remember that the normal number of chromosomes in man is twenty-three pairs, making a total of forty-six. If, in addition to the translocation chromosome (actually two chromosomes), an individual had forty-five other chromosomes, his cells would contain the genetic information usually contained in forty-seven separate chromosomes. Anomalies, therefore, would occur. But if an individual with a translocation chromosome had only forty-four other chromosomes, his cells would contain the genetic information usually contained in forty-six separate chromosomes; anomalies, therefore, would not be likely to occur. For example, mongoloid children born to older mothers usually have Down's Syndrome caused by the presence of an extra chromosome. When, however, a child with the same syndrome is born to a young mother, most likely a translocation of chromosomes accounts for the anomaly. If translocation is present, as opposed to the more common situation in which it is not, the chromosomes of the parents should be studied. If either parent also has a translocation, chromosomal studies may be recommended before they attempt another pregnancy.

Since the determination of chromosomal constitution before birth is now possible, much attention has been focused recently on the possibilities of diagnosing genetic errors before birth. But since those types of chromosomal errors that result in a child with anomalies are not common, routine examination of the chromosomes of every unborn child would be neither wise nor practical.

Diagnosis before birth requires amniocentesis, a technique by which doctors withdraw some of the fluid and cells that surrounds the fetus. But this technique, already described in Chapter 4, cannot be performed safely before the thirteenth week of pregnancy. Usually the cells must be studied by special techniques that may require as long as six weeks for completion. Moreover, there are presently only a very few disorders in which diagnosis before birth is possible and unfortunately there are still no methods available for treating a defective unborn child. However, the recognition of certain defects and performance of a therapeutic abortion can save you and your wife much hardship.

Problems with Genes

Birth defects may result at times even when the chromosomes appear normal. In such cases the abnormality is with the genes. Chromosomes, you will recall, are in pairs. Because paired chromosomes each consist of genes located in a definite linear sequence, one by one like the pearls on a necklace, it is logical that each gene has a mate, technically called an allele, on the opposite chromosome of the pair.

Sometimes a gene undergoes a change and as a result no longer functions in its usual manner. We refer to this as a mutation. Mutation may occur in one or in both genes of a pair. If mutation in just one gene of the pair produces a recognizable effect such as a birth defect, we say that the mutation is "dominant." Dominant disorders tend to be passed from generation to generation. Huntington's chorea and achondroplastic dwarfism are examples of dominant disorders. If one parent has a dominantly inherited condition, chances are 50 percent that any expected child will have the same condition. Autosomal dominant disorders—disorders in which the genes are not on the X or Y sex chromosome—cannot be diagnosed before birth.

If mutation must occur in both a gene and its mate in order to produce a recognizable effect, we say that the disorder is recessive. Autosomal recessive disorders tend to be more severe than dominant disorders and usually appear only in situations in which both husband and wife have a mutation of one gene at the same site. In such circumstances chances are 25 percent that an infant will have the disorder. Some autosomal recessive conditions include cystic fibrosis and phenylketonuria (PKU). Other recessive conditions involve failure to produce an enzyme. A few of these rare enzyme disorders can be predicted before birth by the performance of chemical studies on fluid and cells taken by amniocentesis. But once again, because recessive conditions are quite rare, routine evaluation of all fetuses to determine the presence of very few diagnosable disorders is not practical. If you have given birth to a child with an enzyme defect, however, amniocentesis may be indicated for purposes of predicting whether subsequent children will be affected. Your pediatrician should be consulted if you are not sure.

Certain recessive disorders result from mutation of genes on the X sex chromosome. Because a female has two X chromosomes, a mutation on only one of the X chromosomes would not cause a recessive disorder, assuming the paired gene on the other X is normal. A recessive mutation on only one X chromosome would produce an effect in a male, however, because there is only one X chromosome and there would be no "normal" allele to "oppose" a mutant gene. Disorders caused by mutations of genes located on the sex chromosomes are not necessarily concerned with sex, but with such disorders as hemophilia and some forms of muscular dystrophy.

Amniocentesis might be indicated, on the other hand, if hemophilia or similarly inherited disorders are present in the mother's family. If they are, the mother might be a carrier of the disorders. If she is a carrier, female children would not be affected but male children could be affected. It would therefore be useful to know the sex of the unborn child.

Finally, there is another group of genetic disorders about which we know very little. These disorders are probably caused by a combination of mutation at many gene sites and environmental factors. Some of the commonest types of birth defects fall into this group of genetic disorders. They include most forms of congenital heart disease, club feet, hare lip, cleft palate, congenital hip dislocation, and spina bifida. We cannot predict before birth whether these disorders will be present.

In summary, abnormal development may result from errors in the number or in the structure of chromosomes, from gene mutation involving one or more sites, and from environmental causes such as viruses and drugs. Although the prospects are promising for eventually diagnosing many congenital disorders before birth, there are presently only a few situations in which prenatal diagnosis is both indicated and possible. These include problems involving chromosomal translocation, certain rare recessive enzyme defects, and genetic disorders in which only one sex is usually involved. Many scientists are working in this area, and advances should enable us in the future to diagnose still other disorders before birth.

CHAPTER 6

The Rh Factor

Suppose you and your wife learn that she might give birth to a so-called Rh baby. Be reassured that there is no reason for either of you to be unduly concerned! An understanding of this rare medical problem should dispel or at least allay most of your fears.

The Rh factor was so named because it is a substance found in the red blood cells of *all* monkeys of the rhesus family. This same substance has been identified as present in the red blood cells of almost all humans. But the mere fact that it is missing in some of us is the crux of the problem. Among white people, 15 percent lack this Rh factor; only 5 percent of black people lack it and only 1 percent of Orientals. Those people who lack the Rh factor are called Rh-negative and those who have it are called Rh-positive.

Doctors are concerned only with that small group of Rh-negative wives whose husbands are Rh-positive for *only* this combination can have so-called Rh babies. Moreover, only one in one hundred of the babies from this husband-wife category will become an Rh baby. Obviously, since the odds for such a baby are so low, this medical condition is labeled rare. Furthermore, it is important to remember that there is no risk to the mother; this problem affects only the baby. And even those few babies who are affected by the Rh problem generally survive as normal healthy babies.

What Causes the Rh Baby

When the father is Rh-positive and the mother is Rh-negative, the fetus often inherits the Rh factor from its father, and its blood is therefore Rh-positive. There continues to be no problem to this fetus until some time during the pregnancy, and most frequently during delivery, when some of the fetal Rh-positive red blood cells enter the mother's blood stream.

As soon as this happens, the Rh-negative blood of the mother will automatically develop antibodies against the incompatible Rh-positive red blood cells of her baby. This normal reaction is the appropriate way her body responds to protect her by destroying the incompatible blood cells entering her body.

But at this point your doctor must exercise concern. Under his watchful eye, the baby can be removed from the potential danger that exists. As soon as the maternal level of Rh-antibodies becomes high enough, they in turn can cross the placental attachment, enter the fetus and, thereby, destroy its red blood cells causing Rh disease or, as it is otherwise known, hemolytic disease of the newborn (erythroblastosis fetalis).

The Rh Baby Can Be Saved

At intervals during the pregnancy, the doctor will draw small samples of your wife's blood and have it screened for Rh antibodies. If none are found in the final test, which is made during the eighth month, the chances are just about zero that there will be any trouble. It is also worthwhile to know that a first child is rarely threatened. Furthermore, ample evidence shows that most Rh-negative women married to Rh-positive men can expect to have two, three, and even more babies without fear of Rh-disease.

Now suppose the worst, that Rh antibodies are detected in your wife's blood. Your doctor will follow a precise procedure to protect the baby. He will order an Rh titer or indirect Coombs test to determine exactly how strong the antibody level is in the mother. If the antibody titer is high, and the doctor fears the baby is in danger, he will have an amniocentesis done.

You will recall that this is a procedure in which some amniotic fluid surrounding the baby is withdrawn by means of a very fine needle puncture through the abdominal wall of the mother. When examined, this fluid can give a very accurate indication of the baby's condition. In this case the amount of jaundice pigment (bilirubin) in the fluid tells how severe the condition is. Red blood cells, when they are destroyed by the Rh antibody, break down into bilirubin. Obviously the more bilirubin present the greater the amount of red blood cell destruction or anemia. If the doctor resorts to examination of the amniotic fluid at regular intervals, the inference is also obvious. He is using the laboratory tests along with his clinical judgment to determine the appropriate and safe time for delivery of the baby.

Early delivery is frequently advised for infants with Rh disease. When the decision to deliver before term is made, adequate facilities for care of the premature infant as well as the necessary equipment for carrying out an exchange blood transfusion must be available. The doctor will keep an eye on the situation making all the advance preparations that science has developed to treat the baby immediately after birth.

The Rh Baby Is Born

Following birth, the doctor will immediately submit samples of the baby's blood to the laboratory to determine the number of antibodies present, the amount of bilirubin, and the degree of anemia which resulted from red blood cell destruction.

If the amount of bilirubin present reaches a certain specified level, and/or the baby is severely anemic, an exchange transfusion is performed. The purpose of the exchange is three-fold:

1. to decrease the amount of circulating bilirubin thus preventing severe jaundice and subsequent brain damage;
2. to correct the anemia, and
3. to remove the offending antibodies.

During the exchange transfusion, the baby's Rh-positive blood is removed and replaced with equal amounts of Rh-negative donor's blood. Obviously, Rh-negative blood is selected because it will not be broken down by the Rh antibodies acquired from the mother, now present and still circulating in the baby's blood.

More Is Done to Reduce the Rh Hazard

In rare instances a fetus may be so severely affected with Rh disease that it will die in the uterus at a stage of pregnancy too early for a safe preterm delivery and exchange transfusion.

But the refinement in amniotic fluid analysis and other tests to accurately predict severe fetal involvement led Dr. A. W. Liley of New Zealand to try intrauterine blood transfusion via the fetal abdomen. This rare procedure can be done by specialists after serial amniotic fluid analysis has shown the baby to be severely affected prior to a safe time for delivery. So far, in carefully selected cases, this procedure has saved nearly fifty percent of the fetuses.

Another exciting advance is the recent discovery of the vaccine RhoGAM for the prevention of hemolytic disease of the newborn or Rh disease. If your Rh-negative wife has not been sensitized to the Rh factor by a previous pregnancy or by transfusion or blood injection, this sensitization now can be prevented in almost 100 percent of the cases. Within seventy-two hours after delivery your wife is given an injection of 1 cc of RhoGAM, a specially prepared gamma globulin containing a high concentration of Rh antibodies. Not only will these antibodies provide protection against the baby's incompatible Rh positive red blood cells which may enter the mother's blood stream at delivery, but RhoGAM prevents the mother's body from producing her own permanent antibodies. You will recall that it is the latter which can be fatal to the fetus; RhoGAM antibodies do not destroy the fetus's red blood cells.

The important thing for all expectant fathers in this situation to do is relax and help your wife relax. Don't anticipate the worst when the odds are so low and the treatment, when necessary, is so frequently successful. Think positively and anticipate a healthy baby!

CHAPTER 7

You're Neither Too Young
Nor Too Old

To those who don't want children, there is never an ideal age to have them; to those who do, any age is best. Since the die has already been cast in your case, you might as well reconcile yourself to the fact that you are going to become a father when you are about nine months older than you are right now. Of course, if you are a teenager or a septuagenarian, you may face some special problems; but others have faced them, solved them successfully, and found that fatherhood at any age can be happy, exciting, and rewarding.

The Best Time

Physiologically, the human male is capable of becoming a father from puberty, which starts at about the age of thirteen, until the so-called climacteric, placed by some doctors at seventy, eighty, or even older, and whose existence other doctors deny completely. Although there has been much study and even more argument on the influence of a father's age on the physical and psychological welfare of his child, the consensus seems to be that there is none. History abounds with the names of distinguished men and women whose fathers were in their late teens or early eighties when their prominent children were born.

In most cases, however, the age at which a man becomes a

father is about the same as the age at which his wife becomes a mother, and in this area some facts are pertinent. In many instances, the older a woman is when she has her first baby, the longer her labor is likely to be. Contrary to popular ideas, the maternal and fetal risks involved in child-bearing past the age of thirty-five are only slightly higher than they are before the age of twenty. Most obstetricians agree that no couple need shun parenthood for this reason. With good medical care, the older woman can look forward confidently to a healthy pregnancy, a safe and comfortable delivery, and a normal baby. Even the slight statistical increase in congenital abnormalities among children born of older mothers can be explained by factors other than age alone, such as the presence of diseases that may come with the years. These too, can be recognized in advance and can usually be controlled so that the hazard to the child will be minimal. Indeed, nature seems determined to compensate for the reduced fecundity of those who decide to have children late in life by making it easier for older women to produce twins. So we can say that from the point of view of health—yours, your wife's, your child's—the age at which you become a father is relatively unimportant.

Are You Ready?

More important than age is your general attitude toward life and toward your wife, your marriage and particularly your unborn child. If you have avoided becoming a father because you don't really love your wife, because you are unhappily married, or because you don't want to be bothered with children, chances are that the pregnancy was unintentional, at least on your part, and that you'll resent both it and the baby. If this is the case, and if you cannot work out the problem for yourself, you ought to seek professional help as soon as possible, both for your own sake and for the sake of the other two human beings involved. On the other hand, the baby may be just what you wanted without realizing it.

One obstetrician was seriously concerned when a twenty-three-year-old patient tearfully told him that her husband was fifty-eight and an enormously busy and successful industrialist who had little time for his home. Furthermore, he had two children by an earlier marriage who were older than his wife, and three grandchildren. This woman was deeply in love with her husband, but feared he did not love her as much, and that this pregnancy, which she thought he had not wanted, would destroy their marriage. The doctor told her there was nothing to be done about it now and advised her to tell her husband that he was about to become a father again. The husband's reaction was a complete surprise. He had long wanted another child but had been afraid to talk about it with his young wife. Certainly, he had not been spending very much time at home, for in addition to his business responsibilities, he loved to visit his grandchildren and play with them, and he felt that his wife resented these attentions. Now that he would once more have a young child of his own, the house would no longer be so terribly quiet and life would be full of fun.

Now, or Never?

There are problems, however, that worry older fathers and that do have some validity. A question frequently raised is how the man who becomes a father at sixty will react ten years later, when his son or daughter is at one of the most exasperating stages of growing up and he is—the fact must be faced—an old man. Will he be able to provide the fatherly companionship and guidance that every child needs? Will he be so far removed from the joys and sorrows of youth that he will be unable to understand them? Will his child, indeed, resent the presence of an old man as a father? Questions such as these are difficult to resolve. Nevertheless, if they are faced honestly and courageously, some of them can be answered. A distinguished doctor illustrates just one of many possible approaches to this problem by telling of his own experiences when he became a father at the age of sixty-one. A busy professional career had left him little time to pursue other interests that once had attracted him. Since he now had enough money to take care of himself and his family for the foreseeable future, he decided he would begin to learn about the many things the world offered outside the field of medicine. During his daughter's early years, the physician took keen delight in building wooden toys and even designed a few new ones. When the child entered school, the father grasped the opportunity to renew his own boyhood interest in history and geography. Later, when the little girl took up the piano, he determined that he would fulfill a lifelong ambition to play the violin, but settled for the clarinet when he found that his fingers were too stiff to negotiate scales on a stringed instrument. This man had no trouble whatever in getting on with his young child, for he grew up a second time along with her. Indeed, he was far happier with his young wife and child than many men who may be closer in age to the rest of the family, but have neither the time nor the interest to concern themselves with what the others want to do.

Perhaps the most serious problem that bothers older fathers, even though they may not express it openly, revolves around the fear that they may not live long enough to enjoy the child or to provide for all of its needs. There is no real solution to this problem. There is small comfort in knowing that the life expectancy of American men has risen considerably over the last few decades, and that it is likely to go even higher in the future. Nor does it help to realize that no human being can be sure that he will be alive tomorrow, whether he is seven, or seventeen, or seventy. Nevertheless, you can take two precautions. First, take this opportunity to have that complete physical examination that you have been putting off, and follow your doctor's advice. Second, make every possible provision for your family's welfare that you can. Chapter 22 in this book, on financial planning, ("Babies Are Expensive"), will give you some very definite and practical suggestions.

Plans Must Be Made

The very young father does not ordinarily worry about his health, although he, too, might well see a doctor after his wife has seen her obstetrician for the first time. However, he might have other serious problems of his own. The first of these is usually financial and will be discussed in Chapter 22. It might be pointed out here that more youthful marriages founder on the rock of money than on any other single hazard.

Some young husbands and wives put off having a family because they feel they cannot afford one. Other couples approach parenthood with too little sense of responsibility, hoping they will muddle through or that their own parents will come to the rescue. Both extreme attitudes are reflections of immaturity and are dangerous. The couple who defer having children until financial security is assured, or until a better apartment can be secured, or until the husband has completed his education, or for any one of many other reasons, is not really facing the fact that they probably do not want to have children at all. Such a couple is likely to face a life of frustration especially if one of them openly or secretly wants children. The couple who leap into parenthood without giving any heed to the financial burdens it brings could be in equally grave danger. The money problem may become so serious that it will take all the joy out of having a baby. Some fathers and mothers are so overwhelmed by their problems that they irrationally blame the child for their predicament and grow to resent it. Part of the solution for both types of couples lies in recognition of the underlying problems, conscious effort—with professional help if necessary—to overcome them, and careful planning.

Most very young couples, however, make excellent parents despite all the difficulties involved in early marriage. Indeed, while experts in the field of family counseling never urge youthful husbands and wives to solve their marital problems by having a child, many of them feel that the arrival of a baby, even when initially unwanted, frequently helps.

Problems Can Be Solved

The head of a social service agency in a large city cites the case of a youthful marriage that was rapidly breaking up. The husband was a graduate student in engineering, and his wife worked as a secretary to support both of them. She secretly resented the necessity of supporting a man, and he had profound guilt feelings about depending on a woman. The social worker recognized that their marital difficulties were based on deep-seated emotional problems, traceable to their own childhoods, and had almost abandoned hope of preventing a divorce. She became even more concerned when one of her field workers reported that the young woman was pregnant. To her surprise, however, the couple seemed happier than they had ever been when she saw them on their next visit to her office. The wife spoke in glowing terms about her job, boasting about the things she would be able to do for her baby with the money she was now saving with their newly revised budget. The husband, too, was now enthusiastic about his studies, and was doing so well in them that one of his professors had recommended him for a part-time job with a local firm. Furthermore, they were working together to prepare for the new baby. He had built a partition to create a new room in their small apartment—the first bit of practical engineering he had ever performed. She had learned to sew, and was making curtains for the new room as well as all the little things that a new baby needs. They felt they had a new purpose in life. Both became more mature, more ingenious, and more responsible. Most important for their future happiness, they had learned that a marriage can grow as a result of adversity, that human beings derive great joy from doing things for each other, and that a married couple finds their greatest happiness together in planning and working for a child.

You are, then, neither too young nor too old. For in this area of life, as in many others, age is not counted by years but by spirit. If you and your wife are parents at heart, this is precisely the right time to have a baby—your first or your tenth.

The "Artificial" Baby

Carrying a baby for nine months does not make a woman a mother any more than fertilizing a woman's egg makes a man a father. Most of us realize that parenthood consists of sharing the joys and problems of raising a child. A couple can adopt a newborn and become parents in every way except the physical sense. Or the couple can decide to have artificial insemination.

This process is known as AIH for artificial insemination homologous (from husband) or AID for artificial insemination from a donor. Many doctors in clinics throughout the country are helping couples produce an offspring by utilizing either a "sperm bank" where semen is frozen, kept at −190 degrees Centigrade, and used as needed. At times fresh donors are required when the bank cannot match the husband's genetic features; as a rule these are medical students selected by the doctor in the hospital doing artificial insemination. Neither the student nor the couple involved know the identity of each other.

Some of the semen is ejected into the area of the woman's cervix with a syringe, the remainder put into a small plastic receptacle and left in the vagina to be removed by the woman after eight hours.

It is estimated that approximately 20,000 women become pregnant each year after being inseminated with sperm from their husband, from a donor, or preferably with a combination of both when the husband's semen is only partially inadequate. Many couples prefer AID to adoption despite the number of potential problems that could arise. Many say they love a baby from the wife's body more than one they might adopt. Others argue that despite the population problem they have the "right" to at least one child.

However, there are a number of legal angles which have not been completely resolved. Thus, before a couple decides to have artificial insemination, they should discuss the matter with their lawyer as well as with their physician. The following questions have arisen: "Is the procedure lawful?" "Is the child conceived by AID legitimate?" "Is it fraudulent or illegal to execute a birth certificate that does not divulge that the mother's husband is not the child's natural father?" "Does the donor have any obligation to the child?" "Is the child an heir of the mother's husband's ancestors?" "What is the legal relationship between an AID child and a naturally conceived child of the same mother and husband?" "Might a couple denied the privilege of adopting a child circumvent adoption laws by resorting to AID?" "If a woman were inseminated without her consent, would the physician, husband, or others be guilty of rape?"

The American Medical Association's spokesmen believe, as do most authorities, that in states with absence of a specific statute forbidding AID, the procedure is not a crime.

Elective Abortion

With the partial liberalization of the abortion laws in many states for certain indications and the practically complete freedom to have an abortion up to twenty-four weeks of pregnancy in New York State, a new aspect to expectant fatherhood has arisen. Whereas prior to the new legislation concerning abortions it was illegal to have an abortion and a physician could only counsel you and your wife as to a therapeutic abortion, you now legally have the choice of having an elective abortion. Do not make a decision hastily. Discuss your reasons with your physician, religious adviser or social worker and then think about it some more. Many obstetricians know of instances where their patients had illegal abortions done in the past and then were unable to conceive several years later when they wanted more than anything to become pregnant.

CHAPTER 8

Will You Be a Good Husband and Father?

Whether or not you will be a good husband and father depends on the kind of human being you are now, and that was largely determined many years ago, during your infancy, childhood, and adolescence. It is probably too late to make basic changes in your personality, but this may be a good time to take a long and honest look at yourself, learn how to magnify your virtues and minimize your defects, and perhaps even seek some kind of professional advice if you feel that this is necessary. You are going to play a mighty important role in rearing your child and helping your wife through the major experiences of pregnancy and childbirth. Both your hidden attitudes and overt behavior are likely to have a profound and permanent influence on your marriage, on the immediate and future health and welfare of your wife, on many aspects of your child's growth and development, and on your own happiness.

Happy Sons, Good Fathers

How you reacted on first learning that you were about to become a father may provide some good clues that will help you gain a deeper understanding of yourself. For example, some men are excessively joyful and enthusiastic, so much so that they inadvertently neglect their wives. One woman plaintively told her obstetrician that her husband scarcely took time to give her a cursory kiss of congratulations before rushing to telephone the good news to his mother about his great plans for his "son's" education and career. He was always too busy to accompany his wife to the doctor, because he was either at the office making enough money to assure the child's future or with his college buddies boasting about the scholarly football star who would grace the halls of their alma mater come nine months and eighteen years. As this woman's pregnancy went on, her husband spent less and less time with her because there were so many things to do for the child. Finally, the obstetrician decided to take matters into his own hands. He telephoned the husband and insisted that he come to see him—alone! In plain terms the doctor made clear that the most important person in his family right now, even from the viewpoint of the unborn child, was the wife. The doctor knew he could do little to change this man who was preparing to relive his own unsatisfactory youth through his child, but he warned the husband that his wife's health was suffering as a direct result of his neglect. This could jeopardize both her and the baby, and, if he persisted in his behavior, all three members of the family might be in for a lifetime of trouble and unhappiness. He also hinted, as gently as possible, that the son might turn out to be a daughter.

It is perfectly natural for a man to be joyful and enthusiastic when he finds out that he is to become a father. He should, however, consider the true reasons for his response. Is he happy not only for himself, but for his wife, for the fruition of their marriage, for the child in whose development they will share but who will eventually grow up and want to lead an independent life? Then he will probably be a good husband and father. If, on the other hand, he sees in his unborn child only an opportunity to "get even" for the things he missed, to acquire social or financial status denied to him, or to boast of his devotion and self-sacrifice as husband and father, he could fail in both roles unless he makes a conscious effort to change. There are a few positive things he can do. First, tell himself the truth. Then, discipline himself to think of his wife and their child even though the first thoughts that pop into his head concern only his needs and desires. Finally, he can deliberately plan to give more time and attention to his wife and, later, to both her and their child. If this makes him uncomfortable or unhappy, he must realize that time and attention given to his family are among the many unpleasant consequences and responsibilities of maturity. If his discomfort or unhappiness becomes intolerable, he should seek the advice of a doctor, a clergyman, or someone else professionally equipped to cope with his problem.

It Takes All Kinds

At the other extreme are the men who go into a depression when they learn that they are about to become fathers. This reaction may take many forms, but frequently is manifested by over-concern with the wife's health during her pregnancy and later by constant worry about the child's physical condition. One obstetrician tells of a husband who manifested resentment of his wife's pregnancy by suddenly changing from an easygoing to an aggressive person. It was he who selected the doctor and telephoned to make the first appointment. While his wife sat meekly in a corner, he plumped himself down at the desk and answered all the questions dealing with symptoms and medical history, including date of the last menstrual period. Thereafter, he attempted to dictate how everything should be done. One snowy night, the obstetrician received a message to call this husband, who said that his wife had given birth an hour before, but he was having a little difficulty in delivering the afterbirth. The doctor dashed to his patient's home to be greeted by a whispered injunction to be quiet, because the wife was asleep. The husband had managed to deliver the placenta and the physician could go home. The doctor, however, refused to leave until he had examined the new mother. The bedroom, he was amazed to find, had been completely equipped as a delivery room. The husband had planned all along to deliver his own wife. He had come along on every one of the prenatal visits not because he was concerned with his wife's welfare, but to learn as much as possible about the mechanics of labor and delivery. The only thing that he had overlooked were eye drops for the baby. He asked the obstetrician to administer these—and to sign the birth certificate.

Can You Share?

Some degree of jealousy of the unborn child is perfectly normal, but even the rare husband who shows this reaction to an unusual degree can make a proper adjustment. Some overly jealous husbands the obstetrician never sees, for "such matters are for women, not for real men." Others lose themselves in work, play, or even drink. Most doctors concur that this type of man apparently resents the added responsibilities that fatherhood will entail. He fears that his wife will have to divide her love between him and the new baby; that he will no longer have either freedom or money to indulge himself in his own fancies. This kind of man sometimes regrets ever having married. Consciously or unconsciously, he pines for bachelor days and misses the irresponsibility and carefreeness of youth. Can such an immature person ever be a good husband and father? It is difficult, but it can be done—if the man faces the truth about himself honestly, takes steps similar to those suggested for the over-enthusiastic father, and seeks professional help should his marriage threaten to founder.

The so-called normal husband is far more difficult to describe because, as one old-time obstetrician has said, "After almost fifty years of observing several thousand expectant fathers, I still do not know how they should react." Most doctors like to see a husband who is concerned about his wife, but not hysterical; who shows an intelligent interest in her condition and attempts to help as much as he can but does not interfere with the medical expert nor treat his wife as if she were a delicate piece of porcelain; who realizes that his wife is undergoing a difficult period in her life but also recognizes that he, too, must continue to lead a full and happy existence if he is to be a good husband and father. Above all, most doctors like to see a husband who acts naturally.

Be Yourself

Any husband truly in love with his wife will be especially concerned when she is undergoing the emotional and physical stresses that are bound to arise even in the easiest of pregnancies. If you have always been accustomed to talk about such matters with your wife, continue to do so; if you suddenly keep your fears to yourself, she will be the first to recognize the change and worry, too. Specifically, if you will call the doctor about anything that bothers you he will most likely be able to set your mind at ease. One husband grew more and more irritable as his wife approached time for delivery. He became sleepless, lost his appetite, and neglected his appearance. When his wife casually mentioned this to her obstetrician, the doctor asked that the husband see him. The story then came out. His wife was suffering from hemorrhoids, which commonly occur during pregnancy and usually disappear after delivery. She had mentioned this minor complaint to her husband, but he was afraid that the truth was being kept from him. Wouldn't the bleeding cause anemia? Could the baby be harmed? Was the doctor sure that it was hemorrhoids? And then the question that was really bothering him—Was this cancer? The obstetrician was able to reassure the worried husband who then bought flowers for his wife on his way home, ate his first good meal in weeks, slept soundly through the night, and once more became the happy, natural husband that he had always been.

You should behave naturally in other ways as well. It is perfectly all right to cater to some of the strange tastes that your wife may develop during her pregnancy. But don't let her condition force you into doing things that you wouldn't ordinarily do and that finally might lead to resentment on your part. This will only result in trouble for both of you. One woman thought nothing of asking her husband to get out of bed in the middle of night to hunt out an all-night delicatessen so that she could have a special snack she craved. This happened more and more frequently, until the long-suffering husband became irritable. Finally, he rallied enough courage to tell her that if she insisted on indulging her whims at this unreasonable hour, she could just get dressed, take the car, and go downtown herself. After the initial shock, she burst into laughter, for she suddenly realized how silly her demands had been. He immediately felt better, and the tension that had been building up between them was quickly dispelled.

You Can Learn

It is quite normal for a husband to want to learn as much as possible about pregnancy, labor, delivery, and child-rearing, and to make plans for the future security of his family. Many hospitals and other community agencies offer courses to expectant fathers. You may want to attend one, or you may prefer to get most of your information from this book or some of the others listed in the bibliography. You may also find it comforting to talk to a close friend or relative who has undergone the experience of fatherhood. But while courses, books, and friends are helpful, they do not provide all the answers. As an experienced obstetrical nurse said, "It's one thing to know how to select a diaper and to study the knack of applying it properly; it's another thing to do the job without drawing blood from yourself or the squirming baby." You will learn from experience, and you will learn best if you act naturally. For every father, every mother, every couple, every pregnancy and delivery, and every baby is a highly individual thing. If you realize that husbandhood and fatherhood cannot be learned from courses, books, and friends, that you and your wife must handle various situations as they arise, in your own natural way, you are off to a good start.

CHAPTER 9

Life with a Pregnant Wife

Most women enjoy being pregnant. Some are so proud they almost completely change their personalities. This is one of the many areas in which wives can outdo their husbands, and they are not loath to make this clear at every opportunity, openly or by innuendo. You will simply have to recognize your wife's superiority, put up with her boastfulness, and keep absolutely quiet about the several aspects of life in which you and fellow males excel.

You may also gain some solace knowing that there are a few species in which the male does carry the young and deliver them. One of these is the sea horse. The female deposits the egg in the male's abdominal pouch where it is fertilized. After ten days of development, the male goes into labor and delivers up to twenty or more tiny, fully formed babies. He seems to enjoy the process as much as human females enjoy bearing their children.

It's a Pleasure!

And why shouldn't most women love being pregnant? Despite the temporary distortion of their figures, they usually bloom physically and emotionally in every way. They are in good spirits most of the time. Their complexions become transparent and rosy, their eyes shine brightly, they carry themselves, as well as a protruding abdomen allows, with an aura they never had before and will seldom have again. Manufacturers of maternity garments are well aware of this. No longer do designers strive to conceal the pregnant figure; instead, they create dresses, slacks, shorts, even bathing suits and evening gowns, calculated to show it off and to make it as attractive as possible. When your mother was pregnant, she did her best to hide not only her figure but herself. Your wife will do her best to show both off. Furthermore, you ought to encourage her. While it is not a good idea to cater to her every whim, especially in the matter of foods, you ought to do everything you can to help her remain attractive and lead her customary social life. Every pregnant woman openly or secretly fears that she may lose appeal to her husband, and this fear can be the source of real difficulty.

One woman had been extremely happy on her first few visits to the obstetrician but became more and more depressed as the months went on. The doctor was concerned about her emotional state, as well as the effect of resultant sleeplessness and loss of appetite upon her physical condition. Tactful questioning revealed that the husband had been spending less and less time with her. Fortunately, the physician knew that this man was an accountant, and that the later stages of his wife's pregnancy unfortunately coincided with the tax season. Reminded of this, the woman admitted that throughout her marriage she had seldom seen her husband from January through April; things were no different now. This reassured her that her husband still loved her. The doctor also called the man privately and advised him to give up a few accounts, if necessary, so that he could spend a little more time with his wife.

The hypersensitivity that caused this woman to misinterpret her husband's customary and hitherto perfectly acceptable behavior was not at all unusual or abnormal. The next chapter will provide a brief account of the physiology of pregnancy, but suffice it to say here that the developing baby is growing within your wife's body; that it is, in a sense, a parasite living off her body, that the entire glandular complex is affected by this new state; and that the function of many of these glands is intimately related with the nervous system and the psyche.

Enjoy the Time

While most women are proud of the pregnant figure, some dislike it or are ashamed of it. In a few, the bulging abdomen can cause actual physical discomfort. During the final months of pregnancy, there may be some difficulty in walking, sitting, or standing. Some women even have trouble in maintaining their balance. If your wife has any of these troubles, her obstetrician will give her good advice, but you too can be of real help. Of course, you won't tease her or try to "kid" her problems away. And there are things that you can do on the positive side. Make sure that she has a comfortable, hard-backed chair and a small footstool at home, and get her a light, firm, attractive cushion that she can use in the car. When you are walking together, unobtrusively take her arm, especially when crossing streets or climbing stairs. If her back hurts, rub it gently. Help out with the unavoidable household chores, and encourage her to neglect those that are relatively unimportant.

Even before she knows she is pregnant, it is possible that your wife may suffer from one of the minor, but nonetheless real, annoyances of pregnancy—morning sickness. Only some 50 percent of pregnant women have this type of nausea, and it usually disappears after the first few months. Nevertheless, when it does occur, it is no laughing matter. Have her ask the doctor about it. He will give her advice on how to control this condition, and he may prescribe medication. You must cooperate. Don't belittle your wife's symptoms and don't try to jolly her out of them. She feels miserable enough without any misguided attempts at humor or any strong-arm "brave-girl" techniques. Instead, try taking her out to dinner now and then. A walk in the fresh air, followed by a pleasant meal that she does not have to prepare, may provide some relief. This is one of the many emotional aspects of pregnancy. They are real, and the sympathetic and understanding husband can do much to control them.

As the growing uterus presses upon the other organs near it, your wife may suffer from even more annoying symptoms, none of which is really serious. For example, she may have heartburn, constipation, gas pains, or urinary frequency. At home and alone, these symptoms present no problem, but they can prove quite embarrassing in other places or in company. A little planning and consideration on your part will help. Learn to sense your wife's impending discomfort; then you can suggest going home early, using the excuse that you are tired or have an unusually busy day ahead of you.

Some Problems

Some of the symptoms occasionally associated with pregnancy should be managed by the doctor, but even with these you can help. A few women suffer from varicose veins, hemorrhoids, skin rash, insomnia, faintness, shortness of breath, and some other minor but nonetheless real annoyances. Encourage your wife to mention these to her obstetrician, and then help her to follow his advice.

Weight Control

Perhaps the most common—and the most serious—complication of pregnancy is obesity caused by overeating. Statistics have been presented recently which indicate that excessive weight gain in a woman pregnant for the first time, primigravida, is associated with a greater incidence of prolonged labor, Caesarean section, prematurity, and toxemia. These increases are great enough to warrant a program of weight control in all women, not only before the start of pregnancy but also during its entire course. Here you can be of great assistance. At the first visit, the obstetrician probably gave your wife a diet carefully designed to meet her individual needs and to provide adequate nutrition for mother and baby without causing the former to gain excessive weight. If you insist that your diet remain completely unchanged, your wife is going to find it extremely difficult to adhere to the one prescribed for her.

One woman who was gaining too much weight during her pregnancy insisted to her obstetrician that she was following her diet rigidly. She never ate any of the rich foods that her husband insisted on having and that she delighted in preparing for him. She simply had to taste them while they were cooking—every good chef did that. The doctor explained that these nibbles and sips were just about enough to provide the extra calories that were going into fat and not into baby. Another husband thought that he was being considerate of his wife by taking her out to dinner as often as possible during her pregnancy. However, he expected her to eat salads while he gorged himself with every delicacy on the menu. Only a saint could have resisted such repeated temptation, and the woman began to gain weight until her doctor gave strict orders, not to her, but to her husband. Life will be happier and healthier for both of you if you help your wife to obey her doctor's dietary orders, and if you take the opportunity of your wife's pregnancy to revise your own eating habits.

Emotional Aspects

Perhaps more serious and certainly more annoying than the physical changes and problems of pregnancy are the psychological and emotional ones. In this area, alterations and difficulties may arise in you as well as in your wife. She may be nervous, irritable, moody, and easily moved to tears or laughter. She may spend hours sitting by herself, her face suffused with a smile of inner self-satisfaction, not at all interested in you and your problems. Soon thereafter, she may insist that you take her out for a good time and be resentful if you are too tired to accompany her. Indeed, she may be resentful of you altogether, as the one who was responsible for her predicament and who bears none of the burden of childbearing. No doubt she will have certain definite fears, and a few vague ones, about herself and the baby. Some of these she will express to you, while others she will keep strictly to herself or confide to someone else.

Most of these unnecessary fears and worries are aroused either by an unfortunate previous pregnancy or by the experience of a woman your wife knows or has heard about. They usually involve two major areas: abortion, stillbirth, and congenital abnormalities; and the effect on pregnancy of certain viral diseases such as German measles, common infections, and drugs. Like all problems associated with pregnancy, these should be frankly and thoroughly discussed with the physician.

Keep Smiling!

One husband, whose wife spent every Friday morning at the hairdresser and then visited her mother in the afternoon, knew that he would face serious problems on every Friday night. He soon learned that if he listened patiently, offering comfort and assurance and occasionally suggesting that the doctor was the best person to consult regarding all the difficulties of pregnancy, his wife would soon calm down. He also found that if he came home with a surprise gift or a plan for a movie or some other form of entertainment, he could help his wife overcome this recurrent crisis and preserve his own good humor.

On the other hand, another husband, himself beset with guilt, fear, anxiety, and hostility far beyond that which normally appears in any man whose wife is pregnant, made matters worse by his behavior. He would telephone his wife's obstetrician every Monday morning to report minor and unimportant episodes that had occurred over the weekend. He would also telephone on the day of every prenatal visit, telling the doctor what his wife had done or eaten during the preceding weeks, and admonishing him to keep the call secret. Later that day, he would again telephone the obstetrician to make certain that everything was all right. After three or four months, the doctor noticed that the woman, who had started her pregnancy happy and content, was now coming in with all the old wives' tales and with long lists of questions pertaining to long past pregnancies of relatives and friends. This man unwittingly was intensifying his wife's own real fears, adding new ones and making her prey to every superstition and myth perpetuated by generations of unhappy, uneducated mothers. It was not until the obstetrician had a long talk with this husband that the telephone calls stopped and the wife began to behave normally once again.

Cheer Her Up!

Granted that you have your own worries about your wife and her pregnancy and that you may have had many other trials and tribulations during the day, when you come home at night be prepared to be a good listener and, if need be, a good source of encouragement. Listen to any unprofessional and most often unsolicited advice your wife may have picked up during the day. Any woman who has had a baby feels obliged to advise another who is undergoing the experience of pregnancy for the first time. As your wife repeats some of these stories and bits of information, she will probably be watching expressions on your face and gauging your reactions to them. She may appear to be relating them in jest; she may in fact be waiting for you to assure her that much of what she has heard is untrue. Never be flippant, offhand, or act annoyed, even if you are. It is up to you to lend your wife support and to help her to view herself, her baby, you, and all the tales she hears, in proper perspective.

Another common fear, seldom expressed but frequently revealed in other ways, is that of death. Both you and your wife may suffer from this, especially if you have heard of some particularly harrowing or unfortunate pregnancies and deliveries. If this perfectly natural and normal fear becomes so overwhelming as to be troublesome, it should be given professional attention. Most frequently, however, a talk with a good and rational friend, reading the facts in this book and in others, and especially a brief talk with the doctor will dispel this fear.

A career woman who was pregnant for the first time at the age of thirty-seven would question her obstetrician constantly about various complications of which she had heard during the interval between visits. She would conclude each of these sessions by asking if it would be necessary for her to have a Caesarean section. It was not until two weeks before she was due to deliver that the doctor finally learned her best friend had died after such an operation more than ten years before, and she was in mortal fear that the same thing would happen to her. As mischance would have it, this woman did need a Caesarean section, but being aware of her fears, the obstetrician could assure her in advance and tell her truthfully that the risks involved in this method of delivery are now scarcely greater than those in normal childbirth.

Must You Suffer?

The matter of the overdemanding wife, although mentioned earlier, deserves a little more attention here. There are a few women who feel they are doing society in general and their husbands in particular a great favor by bearing children. In return for this generous sacrifice, they make increasing demands, not only on their husbands, but on every other human being they know or even meet casually. This view is sometimes fostered, wittingly or unwittingly, by a mother or a father, particularly if the pregnant woman was an only child.

As the due date gets closer, the telephone may ring more often, you may have unexpected visits, and you may even become annoyed with the oversolicitous behavior of your mother-in-law. Play it cool! Your wife is probably not too happy with the situation either.

Awaiting a grandchild is also a particularly emotional experience. Try to remember that the mother of your wife has lived through pregnancy and she knows what it is like. So if she doesn't go too far overboard and upset your wife and you with repetitious stories of her own or other complicated deliveries—keep calm! She probably never had any education for childbirth and may not be as calmly nonchalant as you are.

To your mother-in-law your wife is still her little girl, and now her little girl is going to have a baby of her own. Actually, grandmother would like to spare her daughter the whole childbirth bit and do it herself if she could. So when she repeatedly asks, "How is she?" "What did the doctor say?" "How soon?" try to understand her emotional involvement and be kind. Soon she may be the most available and best babysitter you can find—and at the right price.

The father of an only child called his daughter's obstetrician after her very first visit to get the "lowdown" and to fill the doctor in on many things that "she probably didn't talk about." His information included the fact that she had been a delicate child, that she couldn't stand pain, that she had never been in a hospital, that she had married too young, and that her husband was inconsiderate and a poor provider. After each succeeding visit, this father would call and insist he be given all the details of his daughter's progress. Not only was the father obnoxiously annoying, but his daughter caused difficulties by refusing to follow any advice that did not appeal to her—the obvious reaction of a spoiled child. Furthermore, the husband was slowly going mad and bankrupt keeping up with her incessant and unreasonable demands. The poor fellow finally telephoned the doctor to ask him whether it was really necessary for his wife to remain in bed most of the day. He was getting up early in the morning to prepare breakfast and serve it to his wife in bed. Then he would fix an elaborate lunch before dashing off to work. On his return, he would do the marketing, cook dinner, and do all the housework. In the meantime, his wife read magazines, watched television, and ate unusual delicacies she insisted he bring home. On her next visit, the obstetrician casually asked his patient how she spent her days. When she found out that he knew the truth, the woman became livid with rage, told him to mind his own business, and stormed out of the office. He never saw her again and still wonders how the next obstetrician managed the case, and, more important, how the poor baby and husband are making out.

Whether your wife is pregnant or not, you should be considerate of her. However, she should not be encouraged to expect or demand unusual treatment, especially if you can't afford it or it might be harmful to her, you, the child, or your future family happiness. If you feel that your wife is taking advantage of her pregnancy, don't try to set her straight—she may resent it. Talk to her doctor. He is best able to handle the situation, and he will be very happy to do so.

Stay Happy and Healthy!

Finally, take care of yourself, watch your health, take some recreation, and try to get some joy out of your wife's pregnancy. If you have been in the habit of spending one night a week with the boys, don't suddenly abandon this custom, for the resulting resentment will cause trouble all around. As a matter of fact, your wife will probably want to continue to have one night a week when she can visit with her friends or be alone. However, don't suddenly become so busy with either play or work that you completely neglect your wife when she needs you so much. Remember: it is very important, both to your wife and to your child, that you live long enough to complete the job—and this takes many, many years.

CHAPTER 10

Bugs and Drugs

Infections

Although there is still some speculation in medical circles as to which viruses are likely to cross the placental barrier and gain access to the fetus, more information is now available to guide the doctor in the management of a particular situation. Very few illnesses have been associated with damage to the fetus, and those that do cause damage usually do so during the first three months of pregnancy—and then not in all babies. The important thing is for both you and your wife to rely on your doctor rather than on hearsay.

There is no evidence to prove that such diseases as strep throat, staph infections, or diseases caused by most bacteria harm the fetus. This is because the bacteria are large in comparison to viruses and do not cross the placenta. The obstetrician is frequently asked, "Doctor, I have a cold. Can this harm my baby?" Particularly during the past few years, when public awareness of birth defects has increased, has this type of question become a daily telephone routine. Fortunately the answer is, "No you don't have to worry about the baby. Just take care of the cold." A similar response applies to most other infectious diseases.

German Measles

Certain viruses, however, are able to pass through the placenta and affect the developing fetus. One of the best known and most

57

dangerous is the German measles virus (rubella) which may seriously damage the fetus if it is contracted within the first three months of pregnancy. Recent reports have indicated it may also affect the fetus later in pregnancy.

If a pregnant woman is exposed to German measles, and she does not know whether she has ever had it in the past, a simple blood test can be done to determine this. This hemagglutination-inhibition test is rapid, sensitive, and takes the guesswork out of what formerly was a serious dilemma. If antibodies are present in her blood sample, it can be assumed that the woman has had German measles and nothing need be feared from present exposure. She and the fetus are safe because immunity following German measles is long lasting, even after mild illness or a clinically inapparent infection.

If the test is negative, that is if no antibodies are present, it should be repeated in two or three weeks after any exposure to rubella. If the test is again negative, it means the mother has not contracted the virus of German measles during this exposure. But if the rubella antibody is now detected, and exposure occurred during the first three months of pregnancy, therapeutic abortion should be considered. The administration of gamma globulin to susceptible patients following exposure is of questionable value and may only mask infection and fetal damage.

There is now available a rubella vaccine for immunization. This is a live, attenuated vaccine and should not be given to pregnant women since damage to the fetus could result. It is recommended also that routine immunization in adolescent girls and adult women should not be undertaken because of the danger of inadvertently administering the vaccine before pregnancy becomes evident. However, women of child-bearing age may be considered for vaccination when the possibility of pregnancy in the following three months is nil. Some physicians recommend that a good time for vaccination is immediately after delivery. For added safety, a form of contraception should be employed during this period.

Now it is being recommended that the live rubella virus vaccine be given to children after one year of age. Since there is the very slight possibility that a mother could become infected from her child, it would be advisable to avoid pregnancy for three months after the child is vaccinated.

An excellent time to determine whether a woman has had German measles is at the premarital examination when blood is drawn for the routine premarital examination. At this time, a hemagglutination-inhibition test also can be done to determine whether the woman is immune to German measles. If she is not immune, she may elect to be vaccinated for German measles at this time, care being taken that she not become pregnant within the next three months. In over one-half of the women susceptible to rubella but who were vaccinated with the virus, signs and symptoms of rubella (rash, arthritis, swollen lymph glands, malaise, and so on) developed. These symptoms were mild and transient but should be borne in mind if vaccination is to be considered at the time of the premarital examination shortly before a honeymoon. The rash usually develops twelve days after vaccination and the joint pains sixteen days later. Complete recovery from vaccination takes about one month.

In a sample group of women tested prenatally for rubella immunity, 90 to 95 percent were found to have rubella antibodies. It is hoped that vaccination of children will bring the figure to close to 100 percent in the future and remove completely the danger of congenital defects to the fetus from German measles. I have discussed this subject in detail because it is one of the recent important advances in safeguarding the unborn infant, and one of which all parents should be aware.

Smallpox Vaccination during Pregnancy

Husbands sometimes ask if they can take their pregnant wives on a trip to Europe or some other foreign country. If the answer is yes, they request that their wife be given a smallpox vaccination, since this type of vaccination is required for re-entry into the United States. Many physicians are reluctant to give any vaccinations during pregnancy, particularly smallpox vaccine. Although the danger is slight, there have been reports that the disease itself or the vaccine, which contains live virus, can harm an unborn child. Rather than vaccinate a pregnant woman, some doctors prefer to give her a letter for presentation to the authorities on re-entry to the country with an explanation of why vaccination was not done. Vaccination can then be performed after the pregnancy.

Frequently the doctor is asked which drugs or medication are safe to take in pregnancy. Complete information on all drugs is obviously not available. Moreover, if experiments used to evaluate the effect of drugs on animals could be carried out on humans, many difficulties, such as the tragedy that occurred with thalidomide, could be avoided. We know now that large doses of certain hormones, formerly used in pregnancy to prevent abortion, may cause abnormal growths in female infants; their use for the most part has been discontinued. Some antibiotics have proved harmful in pregnancy. Tetracycline and large doses of chloramphenicol may cause abnormalities in the fetus.

As a general rule, the doctor will avoid using drugs in the first trimester unless the need for them is urgent. However, drugs required for critically ill pregnant patients are used, particularly those that have been in use long enough so that their effect on the fetus is known. During pregnancy, no drug, including aspirin, should be taken without supervision by a physician. Any doctor your wife sees, not just the obstetrician, but the internist, allergist, dentist, ophthalmologist, etc., should be told she is or may be pregnant. If she had been taking medication before she became pregnant, she should tell the doctor at her first visit. Some drugs may be safely continued during pregnancy, some may be stopped, and some may have the dose reduced.

It is best to discuss the pills used for heartburn, constipation, allergies, sinus condition, or any other common illness with your doctor and not listen to well-meaning friends or relatives who prescribe what they think is a safe remedy.

Irradiation

The exact dose of X-ray that can be dangerous to the fetus has not been exactly determined. It depends, among other things, upon the area of the body that will be exposed. As a rule, X-ray is avoided in the first three months of pregnancy, but even during this period, the seriousness of the condition determines whether X-rays should be taken.

A question frequently asked the obstetrician is, "Can the dentist

X-ray my teeth?" In routine dental X-ray examinations, there is no direct exposure to the gonads, embryo, or fetus. Therefore, it is safe for the pregnant woman to have routine dental X-rays at any time during pregnancy. But since the mother may be exposed to scattered radiation, the American Dental Association recommends that children and women in the reproductive age, as well as the pregnant woman, be protected by a leaded apron during dental X-rays.

Effect of Unusual Narcotic Drugs on Unborn

Some babies born to heroin-addicted mothers have shown withdrawal symptoms. Several studies have suggested that the so-called "mind-expanding" LSD be seriously considered as a cause of birth defects. The question of whether or not LSD is a mutagenic agent producing changes in the chromosomes which could result in congenital abnormalities has not been completely resolved. One group of investigators showed that in a total of 127 pregnancies among LSD users, 43 percent ended in spontaneous abortion (compared to about 20 percent in the general population). Of the 127 pregnancies, 62 children were born; of these 56 were normal and 6 were abnormal. Since the incidence of such abnormalities in the general population is 6 in 1000, it was eighteen times higher than normal among these drug users.

One very difficult problem in ascertaining the role of LSD in congenital defects lies in sorting out LSD from a wide range of other possible mutagenic agents used. These include coffee and other caffeine drinks, cigarettes, exposure to X-rays, poor maternal nutrition, and drugs used in previous illnesses, including hepatitis and venereal disease. All of the subjects taking LSD had a history of using multiple agents.

CHAPTER 11

Education for Parenthood

As soon as your wife reveals her pregnancy to friends and relatives, she will be inundated with stories about what "other" obstetricians have advised. Furthermore, now that pregnancy and childbirth have become acceptable subjects for living room conversation and popular magazines, and husbands have at last begun to take an interest in subjects hitherto the concern only of their wives, you, too, are likely to receive a good deal of advice from "experienced" fathers. While some of the advice may be good, the best policy is to take up any questions with your wife's obstetrician. You have reposed your confidence in him; he is the doctor responsible for the welfare of both mother and baby; he knows all of the facts in the case, and each case is highly individual.

A Little Learning

One expectant father who took too seriously the advice that he got every morning and evening on the commuters' special spent hours in the local medical library trying to reconcile the conflicting opinions and almost drove himself, his wife, and their doctor into nervous breakdowns before he was forced to change his ways. Every evening he would go home and plague his wife with a newly acquired bit of information and misinformation. When she intelligently refused to harry her obstetrician with these matters, the husband began to call the doctor himself, questioning him persistently and insisting that he follow certain procedures about which he had heard and read. Finally the physician was forced to tell the man bluntly that he would either have to leave all medical decisions in professional hands or find another obstetrician who would be willing to take a case involving more problems with the expectant father than with the expectant mother.

"Natural" Childbirth

Natural childbirth is one subject that has received a great deal of publicity and about which there is much conflicting advice, particularly from laymen. In its broad concept, natural childbirth is an attempt to correlate the physical and emotional aspects of pregnancy and labor so that the pregnant woman can view these functions with less fear and apprehension and with better understanding. The term "natural childbirth" was popularized by the English obstetrician, Grantly Dick-Read, who emphasized that fear and tension resulted in pain to the woman during labor. He was one of the first to attempt to dispel fear and ignorance by a series of lectures and discussions which included demonstrations and a film designed to provide accurate information. He advocated that under normal circumstances childbirth be conducted without analgesia and anesthesia and with minimal medical interference to produce the most desirable effect for the infant. While this may be possible for some women, for a large majority it is neither advisable nor feasible, for childbirth generally is attended by some pain. However, it is true that pain in labor, like all other pain, can be intensified by psychological factors and lessened by the proper emotional preparation.

Perhaps a better term than natural childbirth is preparation for parenthood or educated childbirth. Interest in the psychological methods of pain relief in labor, in contrast to drugs alone, has increased over the past two decades. Most good obstetricians recognize this phenomenon intuitively, and each in his own way supports and conditions his patients to meet the situation in labor. In one New York hospital, about 60 percent of women go through labor with psychological assistance and a minimum of pain-relieving drugs in a manner satisfactory to both them and their obstetrician.

Preparation for Parenthood

Women who wish to prepare for labor are encouraged to take a course in preparation for parenthood given either by the local hospital, by some qualified agency in the community, or by someone recommended by the physician. Most courses teach exercises in relaxation, muscle control, and various types of breathing to be used during labor. More important, they build the woman's confidence in herself and in the dependability, strength, warmth, and skill of the people who will be with her during labor. It is this faith in the doctor, the nurse, and the husband, if he plans to be with his wife during labor and delivery, that is the basis for successful childbirth.

One of the advantages of preparatory courses is that couples find they are not alone in their fears and ignorance of what to expect during pregnancy and labor. Meeting with four or five other couples every week for six weeks creates a feeling of interdependence and eliminates their fears and loneliness. They are all in this together and are helping one another; their feeling of being in the same boat is as important as learning exercises and techniques of breathing. Most new expectant fathers find it hard to go to the first class, but once they get over that hurdle they enjoy it. Talking with other fathers and watching them practice can make you feel less embarrassed and more sure of yourself.

Psychoprophylaxis (The Lamaze Method)

One of the new, rather popular methods to prepare and train for labor and greatly reduce the need for pain-relieving medication is psychoprophylaxis. This method, based on the conditioning principles of Pavlov, was first introduced in the Soviet Union. It was brought to France by Dr. Fernand Lamaze of Paris in 1952 and is now known as the "Lamaze method." In the United States one of Dr. Lamaze's patients, Marjorie Karmel, first wrote about this method in her book, Thank You, Dr. Lamaze. It was further popularized through the efforts of Dr. Irwin Chabon in his book, Awake and Aware, and by Mrs. Elizabeth Bing in her books, Six

Practical Lessons for an Easier Childbirth and *The Adventure of Birth*. And now, many trained practitioners have gone out to practice this method in various hospitals and communities.

In 1959, the American Society for Psychoprophylaxis in Obstetrics was established and numerous branches and affiliates have since been formed in the United States. An increasing number of American women and their husbands are preparing for childbirth by psychoprophylaxis, and the large majority have been enthusiastic about it. Doctors who have attended patients in this method are convinced that for many of these women this is an ideal method of delivery.

The psychoprophylactic method of childbirth is not merely a technique of so-called "natural" childbirth. It is a psychological and physical preparation for childbirth which includes techniques acquired through concentrated effort and hard work on the part of both the expectant mother and her husband. It is a method that provides analgesia achieved by physical means instead of by drug or chemical means. The basic principles of the psychoprophylactic technique of childbirth as described by Mrs. Bing are education, understanding, preliminary exercises, and a technique of special breathing and relaxation during labor. Mothers are conditioned artificially to deal with the known and accepted discomforts of labor.

In addition, the purpose of the lessons is to recondition the expectant mother to create a new center of concentration in the brain, thereby causing the painful sensations during labor to become peripheral and reducing their intensity. The use of chest breathing rather than abdominal breathing is one of the ways in which the Lamaze technique differs from the Dick-Read method of "natural" childbirth.

In discussing psychoprophylaxis in his book, Dr. Chabon says, "Psychoprophylaxis is neither a display of heroics nor a contest against milligrams of injected analgesia. It is a way to be awake, aware and fully participating during childbirth; a way to have for one's very own the childbirth experience." This method differs from that advanced by Grantly Dick-Read in that "psychoprophylaxis does not promise a spiritual uplifting or an automatically improved mother-child relationship as does the Dick-Read method. It offers a mother a way to experience the basic miracle of life, and she can then place her own value judgment upon it. For many women it is a profound emotional experience. For others it is merely a convenient way to have a baby."

Dr. Chabon also refutes the charges that the practitioners of psychoprophylaxis refuse to administer pain-relieving medication to women in labor. "Analgesics can be and are easily and regularly administered in appropriate doses to prepared mothers if and when they are needed." In his experience and in that of many other obstetricians the prepared woman needs less medication in labor than the unprepared woman.

The husband's role in this technique is crucial. Not only must he learn the techniques that his wife learns in the preparation, but he must help her carry them out during labor and delivery. He must be constantly ready to provide both moral and physical support, not only by his own emotional and physical involvement but also by the application of the specific techniques he has learned in class. Many a woman would have been unable to participate fully in the Lamaze method of childbirth had it not been for the support, encouragement, and guidance of her husband. Some hospitals now permit the husband to remain in the labor room. In a smaller, but increasing number of hospitals, he is also permitted in the delivery room to encourage and support her during the actual birth. How to decide whether to be with your wife during labor and delivery will be discussed in the next chapter.

Rooming-in

Together with the increasing interest of many expectant fathers in the details of labor and delivery has come a desire to be taught to share in the care of the child. Some hospitals have rooming-in maternity service in which mothers and babies share accommodations. It gives parents an opportunity to observe and progressively participate in the care of their newborn babies under medical supervision. At one New York hospital, six specially designed modules are provided for rooming-in postpartum care. Each module provides a room which accommodates four mothers and four infants, an adjoining nursery, and a bathroom. In this setting, the newborn is placed at his mother's bedside for a few hours following childbirth, and mother and child remain together for most of the day and evening. However, during the night and afternoon visiting hours, as well as during the mothers' rest periods, babies are returned to the adjoining nursery. An evening hour is reserved exclusively for fathers; no other visitors are permitted at that time. This provides the parents an opportunity to share in the care of their child from the start.

One of the most frequent reasons given by expectant fathers for wanting to participate in preparation for parenthood courses is the desire to learn how to take care of the baby after it comes home. The program described above, as well as modified rooming-in plans, teach both you and your wife how to care for your baby. Both in prenatal courses and after delivery, nurses demonstrate the handling, feeding, diapering, and bathing of your baby, all the things you have never done and want to learn.

This participation by husbands is a far cry from the time when husbands felt their job was done when their wives became pregnant. We know that not every expectant father is psychologically capable of becoming involved in the various aspects of pregnancy, labor, delivery, and infant care. However, those expectant fathers who do show an interest are not "sissics." The great majority of men who participate with their wives in the courses feel they are of considerable help during labor and afterward. The experience is not only rewarding to them but brings them closer to their wives than ever before.

Breast Feeding—Pro

Your wife may ask you whether she should breast feed. What you say and how you say it may be the determining factor in her decision. The following information is offered to aid you in your judgment and to dispel some myths you may have heard.

The size of your wife's breasts is no indication of their ability to produce milk. Some women with large breasts have a great deal of fat or supporting tissue which is not involved in milk production, whereas women with small breasts can produce more than an adequate supply of milk.

Smoking a few cigarettes a day or drinking an occasional cocktail is not harmful for nursing mothers nor does it affect the quality of the milk. Adequate rest and a well-balanced diet are important during the nursing period. However, your wife is not required to have an angel's disposition to nurse successfully. Even if she loses her temper or gets worried or excited at times, this does not usually affect the quality of the milk, although it may temporarily diminish the flow. As soon as she calms down, the flow will return. Then, too, she may be so happy nursing that little things may not upset her, and she may really act like an angel.

Here are some benefits of breast feeding. The mother's milk is always sterile and at the right temperature. Little preparation is necessary, and no formula can duplicate natural milk for essential ingredients of digestibility. Neither breast nor cow's milk contains sufficient iron, but enough is stored in the full-term baby at birth to last for several months. Many physicians are convinced that mother's milk helps protect a baby against some diseases because the baby acquires some of the mother's disease-fighting antibodies during nursing. Breast-fed children are said to have fewer general infections and respiratory infections than bottle-fed babies.

In addition to not having to get up to give your baby the 2:00 A.M. bottle, several other advantages accrue to you when your wife breast feeds. The female body responds to suckling much as it does to intercourse—the uterus contracts, the nipples become erect, and the skin temperature rises. Masters and Johnson found that nursing mothers tended to have a high level of interest in sex and experienced a strong desire to return to intercourse with their husbands as soon as possible.

The wife who successfully nurses her first child usually follows the same course with the rest of her babies, and this has hidden advantages. Nursing is a form of sex education. The older children learn that the breasts are not just a sex symbol, and they are quite pleased when you tell them that's the way they were fed as babies. With sex education taking on increasing importance, the earlier you can start this in your own family the greater will be the benefits to your children.

Recently the view has been presented in psychoanalytic writings and in academic psychology that nursing for the infant is a central event in his life, an active experience, not a passive one, in which his efforts are monumental. Nursing is a compound experience in which actual sucking and intake of food are only one significant part. Whether the child is securely or anxiously held, whether the mother's grip is gentle or rigid, whether he is carefully "heard" or emotionally ignored, all will make for his comfort or discomfort and will influence his later development. Therefore, feeding should be a relaxed, unhurried procedure for both mother and baby. The baby should be spoken to quietly and lovingly as he sucks. These requirements can be met whether your wife breast feeds or bottle feeds your baby.

Breast Feeding—Con

Although the number of women who breast feed their infants in the United States is increasing, less than half of American women do so. In 1970 approximately 75 percent of infants discharged from the hospital were fed commercially prepared formulas. For the past ten years, the frequency of breast feeding has remained about 25 percent. One-half of these infants will continue to breast feed for the first three months of life and one in ten of all infants will be breast fed for at least four months of life. In terms of absolute numbers, about 900,000 infants are breast fed during the newborn period in the United States.

If your wife has decided not to breast feed, don't tell her you would like her to because your mother breast fed you. The type of feeding your wife chooses is one indication of her personality, and it is this personality which influences your child's development just as does your own behavior when you care for him. It must be obvious that no one method of feeding is psychologically best for all mothers in all situations. Who can say that a woman who bottle feeds loves her baby less than one who breast feeds? Yet, for some, breast feeding is a way of extending themselves and manifesting their love to their infant.

Your wife may have heard of nursing mothers whose babies refused to nurse, who thought the baby was not getting enough nourishment, who developed breast abscess or sore nipples, who were annoyed with wearing a nursing bra and absorbent nursing pads all the time, who had to stay home when they wanted to go out, or who had to watch their diet closely. These and other annoyances do occur and the expectant mother will certainly hear about them.

Although cow's milk is different from human milk, millions of babies have thrived on formulas. Manufacturers now prepare formulas which closely resemble human milk and have the minimum requirements of vitamins C and D (human milk does not contain sufficient vitamin D). These prepared formulas do not require refrigeration, can be fed at room temperature, and supply the same "instant service" as does breast milk.

The advantages that accrue to the husband whose wife breast feeds have been mentioned above. However, you may be one of the men who is not happy because your wife has decided to breast feed. Some husbands worry that their wives spend too much time and affection on the new baby, and they feel neglected. These feelings may be exaggerated when the wife breast feeds. A husband may worry that nursing will make his wife's breasts unattractive. Such a worry is based on misinformation. Actually, many men state that sexual attraction to their wives is increased by seeing her breast feed their child.

There are pills or injections of hormones to prevent painful engorgement of the breasts for those women who decide not to breast feed. The final decision to nurse or not to nurse must rest with your wife. She will be doing all the work, and this is one area where you cannot help. She must do it herself! By all means discuss her decision but don't make her feel guilty if she decides not to breast feed. Babies do grow up healthy and happy on cow's milk. There are convincing arguments on both sides. The important thing is to have your wife choose the method that seems most natural and comfortable to her, and one that you approve.

CHAPTER 12

To the Hospital on Time

Every expectant father has nightmares about not getting his wife to the hospital on time. This occasionally does occur, although rarely with the first child, and emergency ambulance assistance is always available by telephoning the police. It need not happen to you if you learn a few things about the onset of labor, and if you take a few simple precautions.

One for the Road

I have mentioned that alcohol may stop the progression of premature labor in certain instances. If you live a long distance from the hospital and are concerned about getting to the hospital before actual labor sets in, give your wife one or two cocktails before you start. This frequently slows labor or stops it entirely for several hours. But remember not to imbibe yourself at this time—you are doing the driving.

The Three Signs

Labor starts with three easily recognizable signals or signs, which are perfectly normal in a pregnant woman at term—that is, at the end of the ninth month. These may appear separately, in combination, or in any order, and should be immediately reported to the doctor or the hospital. You can dial the number, but let your wife describe what is happening herself; she is likely to be less

71

flustered than you are. In any event, she will not be telling her story through an intermediary.

The most dramatic sign, and one that can be frightening if you are not prepared for it, is the rupture of your wife's membranes resulting in a flow of watery material. This means only that the membranous sac which surrounded the baby for nine months has broken. The amniotic fluid, which has cushioned the child against blows and jars, is escaping either slowly or rapidly. This may or may not indicate that labor has started. If it has, there will be rhythmic contractions of the uterus even though your wife may have no actual pains. You can help her recognize these painless contractions by having her lie flat on a bed while you place the palm of your hand on her abdomen. You will feel the muscles become rigid at each contraction. Do not confuse these with Braxton Hicks contractions, which usually begin at about the fifth month and may continue until term. These are very mild and occur at intervals of half an hour or longer. In any case, telephone the doctor and let him decide what to do.

During the last few weeks of pregnancy, your wife may have a discharge of pale pink or dark brown mucus. If this increases greatly in amount and becomes definitely tinged with blood, it indicates that certain changes are taking place in the cervix, or tip of the womb, and that labor may be very near. Again, if your wife is not having pain, help her to feel for painless contractions—and notify the doctor.

Rhythmic contractions of the uterus are the surest sign that labor is starting. They are the means by which the womb pushes out the baby it has harbored. At first these contractions may come at intervals of fifteen minutes or longer, or may have no rhythm at all. They may be completely painless or accompanied by discomfort so mild that it is attributed to gas, intestinal contractions, or movements of the child. Now you can help. Ask your wife where the cramps are, whether they all arise in the same area, and whether they progressively increase in intensity. You can also help her to feel whether her abdomen becomes hard with each pain.

If the contractions disappear when your wife is lying flat, or if they gradually subside in that position, she is probably not in labor. If, however, they persist in any posture, become more frequent and rhythmic, and are accompanied by increasing pain, she is likely to be starting labor. Her doctor will have told her at what point to call him. Women having their first child are usually asked to wait longer than those who have previously given birth. However, most doctors want to be notified if cramps persist for several hours, even though they may be mild and irregular.

After the contractions assume a definite pattern, clock eight or ten of them, counting from the start of one to the start of the next. Also time the duration of each cramp. Write this information down on paper so that your wife will make no mistakes when she talks to her doctor. As labor progresses, the interval between contractions tends to become shorter, and when they become established at about five minutes apart, they are usually associated with some pain and discomfort and last for about thirty seconds each. However, the doctor should be notified before this—when cramps come at eight- or ten-minute intervals.

Although the nature, timing, and other details of labor differ in each woman, as well as with each pregnancy in each individual, it is safe to assume that with a first baby at term, the child will not be born for at least four to six hours after contractions have been established. Let the doctor decide when your wife should go to the hospital. Don't insist on taking her there too early, and don't let well-meaning friends or relatives rush both of you. This may be bad for her morale.

Off to the Hospital

Don't speed! If you have been wise enough to make a "dry run" to the hospital in advance, you will know the best route and be able to estimate the time of the trip. But don't depend on the first trip that you made with your wife when you reserved her accommodations. One husband who did this found that new road construction had caused a detour which was not only lengthy and time-consuming, but took him along streets that were so unfamiliar that he became hopelessly lost and had to call the police for help. As your wife approaches term, pay a little attention to your automobile. Neither your state of mind nor your wife's will be helped if you discover at the critical moment that you are out of gas, that your battery is weak, or that you have a flat tire. Just to be safe, arrange with a neighbor for the use of his car, or ask him whether he would be willing to drive your wife to the hospital if you became ill or otherwise unavailable. In certain communities, there are special taxi services that are altogether safe and comfortingly reliable.

If this is not your first baby, you will need to make careful arrangements to take care of the other children, not only for the few hours when you will be at the hospital with your wife, but for the days when she will not be at home. This is a very delicate problem, because attitudes of brothers and sisters to the new baby are sometimes determined by what happens to them while it is being born. The child who is suddenly snatched from his bed to be summarily sent to stay with a neighbor he doesn't know or a relative he doesn't like is hardly likely to look upon the new baby with kindness. The older children should be prepared for what is coming and consulted on where they are to stay while their mother is having the new baby. Sometimes it may be desirable or even necessary for the husband to take some time off from work. At the very least, he should make it his business to be at home as often as possible, to spend more time with the other children than he ordinarily does, and to show them that he is as interested in them as he is in the new baby.

Most women have prepared large valises to take along to the hospital with them, then worry about what they have forgotten. Here, too, you can reassure your wife. If she forgets her luggage in the hurry of getting out, it will make no difference, for there isn't a thing in it that she could possibly need until after the baby is born. The hospital will insist that she wear one of their gowns, and no other article of apparel will be required or even permitted. There will be ample time for you to bring her frilly nightgowns, bed jackets, hair ribbons, etc. And don't forget books, magazines, playing cards, and other items that may keep her amused. You, too, are likely to have a long wait ahead of you. Provide yourself with reading matter or with work that will keep you occupied.

For some strange reason, a few women grow ravenously hungry as soon as they experience the first signs of labor. Here is one point on which you will have to be firm with your wife. She should have no solid food, and should confine her liquids to a minimum amount of tea or water. The reason for this is that, should she require general anesthesia during delivery, a full stomach involves definite hazards.

When you finally arrive at the hospital, park right at the entrance and get your wife to the admitting desk. You will probably have plenty of time to find a garage or a parking lot later, and cars carrying patients are always permitted to stop in front of a hospital for a reasonable length of time. The admitting clerk will ask your wife a few questions, and then a nurse or an orderly will take her to her room or to the labor floor. Remember that while you are excited and perhaps frightened, so is your wife. Keep your courage up, and she will follow suit. Even if you have made arrangements to be with her during labor, you will not be permitted to join her until later, for she must be undressed, examined, prepared for delivery, and settled comfortably.

CHAPTER *13*

Painless Labor?

Many people are confused about "natural" childbirth and so-called painless labor. Some husbands like to boast that as a result of natural childbirth, their wives had absolutely no pain during labor and delivery. Wives rarely make such claims because they simply are not true. Unless there is deep analgesia and anesthesia during both labor and delivery—this is rarely used and only under the most unusual circumstances—childbirth is generally attended by some pain. It is true that this pain, like all other pain, can be intensified by psychological factors and lessened by proper emotional preparation such as that given in a preparation for labor course or by a sympathetic and perceptive obstetrician. Fortunately, it is also true that nature has provided some degree of amnesia for any pain experienced in childbirth; in the warm glow of satisfaction and pride that almost invariably follows giving birth, mothers generally forget this pain, and most of them are perfectly willing to undertake the experience over and over again. And you and your wife can be certain that modern medical science has provided your obstetrician with drugs and techniques that make child-bearing far less painful than it was a decade ago.

While you and your wife may wish to discuss several types of pain relief with your doctor during your prenatal visits as well as during labor, you will have to leave the selection of a particular anesthetic procedure to him. He will make his decision on the basis of what is best for your wife in her particular condition and in the immediate circumstances, and what is best for the baby. Don't try to pressure him!

Anesthesia

A few years ago, when caudal anesthesia was widely publicized in the newspapers and popular magazines, one husband shopped around until he found an obstetrician who promised that he would use this technique, which involves the insertion of a long, flexible needle into the lowermost portion of the spine. However, neither the husband nor the wife bothered to tell the doctor that she had had a minor spinal operation in childhood which had left virtually no scar. The woman went into the labor room confident that she would feel no pain whatever, but when the moment came to insert the needle, the doctor found that it was impossible. The patient refused other medications and was completely unprepared psychologically for the pain of childbirth.

Although the past quarter of a century has seen great progress in the relief of pain during labor and delivery, an ideal obstetric analgesic or anesthetic, applicable to all patients and completely without hazard, is not yet available. In the early thirties, women were given large doses of scopolamine, morphine, and barbiturates —"twilight sleep" drugs—in the belief that deep sedation and amnesia were the best methods. Some women even insisted on general anesthetics such as ether. However, large doses of these pain-relievers at times produced vomiting or excessive bleeding at delivery in the mother and serious breathing difficulties in the newborn child. Recently, the pendulum has swung to the opposite extreme, and a few women insist they want to endure the pain with no relief whatever. Most obstetricians, however, take a middle position. They use combinations of barbiturates and small doses of narcotics along with some of the newly developed tranquilizers, carefully designed for the individual patient and calculated to keep pain at the lowest possible level consonant with the safety of mother and baby. Experience has shown that timing of the drug and careful selection of the proper combination of agents for a particular patient are more important than the actual drugs used, particularly in the effect on the child. But all decisions in this area and all other medical decisions related to your wife's pregnancy and delivery must be left to the obstetrician. He is aware of all possible procedures, knows the facts in each case, has the training and the experience to exercise judgment, and has experts in anesthesiology and colleagues in his own specialty available for consultation. No matter what you hear, there are some safe things that he can do to help your wife with her pain. Even if he cannot use drug-induced analgesia or anesthesia, he can employ local methods administered by injection or rely on a few whiffs of gas to tide your wife over the most painful moments.

Hypnosis

If your doctor has had special training, he may even want to try hypnosis, which seems to work miraculously well with some women. However, no matter what you have heard from your friends or read in the magazines, no doctor should employ hypnosis if he hasn't taken a thorough course in this technique. Indeed, both the American Medical Association and the American Psychiatric Association insist on such training for any non-psychiatrist who wants to use this method of relieving or eliminating the pain of childbirth. This strict requirement stems from the many instances where injudicious use of hypnosis resulted in grave emotional and psychiatric disturbances.

The following is representative of a case in which hypnosis was effective. The patient was a twenty-two-year-old housewife with no previous pregnancy. She was most anxious to remain awake while giving birth and wanted to witness the delivery without medication or sedation. She felt that the only way this could be accomplished was by hypnosis. Hypnotic training was begun at six and a half months gestation. She was hypnotized twice a month and was taught concentration exercises. Two weeks before the expected date of delivery she was seen for three sessions. Suggestions were given that when labor began, she would not mind contractions no matter how strong they were; she would be totally aware and would be able to cooperate fully with hospital personnel. She was also told to have no fear of the entire procedure, that the labor experience was necessary for childbirth, and that she could look forward to this most desired experience. The patient was comfortable when admitted to the hospital. She had begun self-hypnosis at the beginning of the contractions and was fully cooperative. When contractions were close together, she was taken to the delivery room where she was rehypnotized. Labor progressed uneventfully to delivery of a normal baby. The woman was completely relaxed during the procedure and witnessed the birth of her child.

Hypnosis is not something done to someone. It is a condition or state which the person permits under full guidance and direction of a therapist. It is not a fixed single state, a trance, or a specific condition, but an ongoing fluctuating process. It is not a sleeping unconsciousness as is so commonly envisioned, but rather a feeling of hyperawareness and complete control. Many authorities consider hypnosis simply an altered state of consciousness that can occur to anyone accepting an intense relationship with a therapist who catalyzes and potentiates suggestions for the uncritical acceptance of an idea.

Hypnosis would be an ideal analgesic or anesthetic if more people were able to accept it. Unfortunately, only about 30 percent of women can go through entire labor and delivery solely with hypnosis. Therefore, the woman should be informed that some medication may be necessary. This can prevent a depressive reaction if hypno-anesthesia fails. Nevertheless, most women who have been trained in hypnosis and self-hypnosis have reduced fear and require less medication.

Two authorities on the subject have publicly stated that the inadequately trained hypnotist is more likely to harm than benefit those whom he hypnotizes. To illustrate this point, these experts report the case of an obese housewife who was hypnotized for delivery. She was told to practice concentration exercises at home. When she went into labor, her doctor hypnotized her and the procedure seemed to be completely successful. It developed later, however, that during the periods when her physician was hypnotizing her in preparation for her hypnosis during delivery, she believed that he was making improper advances. During her self-hypnotic states, she planned various ways to keep this imaginary experience from her husband. She was sinking deeper and deeper into a dream world of her own and appeared headed for a collapse into schizophrenia. After delivery, she became paranoid about the physician who had hypnotized her and threatened to bring malpractice charges against him. It took lengthy psychiatric treatment to restore her to mental health. This woman was not a proper subject for hypnosis. Many obstetricians and psychiatrists cite even more serious cases, where the patients actually required hospitalization in mental institutions after they had been hypnotized for delivery by untrained practitioners. Unfortunately, you and your friends who have heard about the miracles of hypnosis in obstetrics have probably not read the medical literature reporting its hazards.

Elective Induction of Labor

Another procedure, useful in certain situations and dangerous in others, has received wide public attention. This is the induction of labor. Here, the doctor sets the time for delivery in advance and administers a drug to start the process. Some husbands and wives really believe that babies can be born by appointment, and they see no reason why their doctor won't do what so many other obstetricians have done for their friends. These friends have assured them that the induction of labor is a routine procedure, and they see no reason why the birth of the baby cannot be timed so that it won't interfere with a vacation or a business commitment. One woman even wanted her doctor to induce labor so that her baby would be born on her wedding anniversary—it would be such a pleasant surprise for her husband!

. The record should be set straight. Not all women can have their labor induced safely. There are a number of situations in which induction can be dangerous. If you try to pressure your doctor into promising that he will deliver the infant at a prearranged time, you are asking him to overlook many safety factors. Although induction can be very useful in uncomplicated deliveries and where special equipment and highly trained medical personnel are available, the procedure is rarely indicated merely for the sake of convenience, and is definitely hazardous under certain conditions which are well known to your doctor. If induction of labor is to be successful, certain rules must be rigidly followed, and nobody but your wife's doctor has the information and the training, experience, and knowledge necessary for proper judgments and decisions.

The medical profession in general, and obstetricians in particular, are glad that people in all walks of life are taking a greater interest in matters of health. They are particularly pleased that husbands are concerned with the difficulties their wives face during pregnancy and childbirth, for they feel that the father should be as deeply involved with every aspect of a baby's birth and development as the mother. However, they are also aware of the fact that in medicine especially, "a little learning is a dangerous thing."

So read all you like, listen to as many stories as you please, even tell a few yourself—but rely on your own doctor and not on advice given to someone else whose situation might be entirely different from yours.

CHAPTER *14*

Do You Belong in the Labor and Delivery Room?

Don't let anyone decide for you if you should be in the labor room during the first stage of your baby's birth. "Anyone" includes your wife, her friend who just had a baby, her mother who may want to run the show, your wife's doctor or other hospital personnel. You and your wife know each other best, and you must make the decision together after considering each other's needs, desires, and personalities. Of course, if your hospital doesn't allow husbands in the labor room, the issue is academic; if it does (and many more are granting such permission), you will want some facts.

You are not a heartless coward if you choose not to be in the labor room, nor a devoted hero if you do. Throughout history and in every society, the role of the father during the mother's labor has varied. Among some primitive tribes, the Campa of the Amazon, for example, the woman continues to work throughout labor and up to the moment of delivery, while the man takes to his bed in the custom known as couvade. The word couvade is derived from the French verb *couver* which means "to brood or to hatch," and was first used to designate a series of related but primitive customs connected with childbirth.

The husband observing couvade goes to bed and pretends to be in labor, sometimes imitating childbirth even to the point of rolling around and groaning. He suffers actual pain and believes he is lessening his wife's suffering and protecting her from harm. By pretending to be her at this critical time, he hopes to direct the influence of evil spirits away from her and onto himself. While in bed, the husband is pampered, fed delicacies, and receives the congratulations of relatives and friends. Often in such primitive societies, the women simply deliver the baby without much fanfare.

In the Middle Ages, it was considered improper and indecent for a man to become too closely involved with pregnancy and childbirth after he had once started the whole sequence of events. The medieval father was permitted to witness labor and delivery only if the child had been conceived out of wedlock. But usually the expectant mother was completely surrounded by women lest any man catch a glimpse of her. Indeed, the male obstetrician is still relatively unknown in less sophisticated cultures, and even in ours, he replaced the midwife only within the last century.

The Rewards

Today, while many physicians believe that a husband should be with his wife during the first stage of labor, some still believe that his proper place is in the hospital waiting room or, even better, at work or in a nearby movie or coffee shop. The former contend that since the birth of a child is the culmination of the closest emotional and physical union that can possibly be achieved the man and the woman should share the experience of birth. The husband benefits by feeling that he is not deserting his wife when she needs him most, when she is literally laboring mightily to bring forth their child—the fruit of the seed that he implanted within her. Thus, he avoids some of the guilt that might otherwise arise, gains a sense of satisfaction at having helped, if only a little, and learns firsthand that childbearing is not at all the gruesome ordeal that his imagination and so much folklore have pictured it to be.

The rewards to the wife are perhaps even greater. No matter how well she has been prepared for the birth of her child, or how eagerly and joyfully she wants it, she'll probably enter the labor room with some anxiety and fear. Not even the best nurse or obstetrician can offer the comfort, assurance, and support that her husband can provide. Even in the most fully staffed hospitals, it is impossible to have someone constantly in attendance throughout the first stage of labor. And when a woman in labor is alone, even briefly, she is mighty lonely. Her husband can give her the companionship she needs, especially when the doctor and the nurse have to leave temporarily. Furthermore, if he has learned a few simple lessons, he can help by rubbing his wife's back during a birth pang, by assisting in the relaxation procedures that she has been taught, by reminding her to breathe properly, by extending a hand she can grip when she needs to, by summoning assistance when necessary, and by performing small but comforting tasks such as swabbing her face with a cool cloth and wetting her lips if she is thirsty.

These advantages are illustrated by the experiences of one couple with the births of their two children. The first time, the husband bluntly refused to be anywhere near the hospital. His wife was very tense and consequently her pain was so severe that she demanded a degree of anesthesia that could have endangered the baby. When she visited the doctor for her second pregnancy, he urged that she and her husband attend a preparation for labor course and encouraged the father to be present during the first stage of his baby's birth. The second labor went smoothly. The mother was so relaxed that she did not require even the lightest anesthesia. To prove that it was the father's presence that was making the difference, the doctor would occasionally ask him to leave, whereupon the wife would become terribly tense and restless and complain of severe pain.

The physicians who object to the husband's presence in the labor room generally accept the validity of their colleagues' arguments but maintain that most husbands just get in the way or cause trouble by increasing the nervousness of their wives or physically succumbing to their own. One obstetrician who had long advocated allowing the husband in the labor room almost changed his mind after an experience that was harrowing at the time, though amusing in retrospect. The couple had taken a preparation-for-labor course and agreed that the husband should be in the labor room. The doctor had his first doubts as soon as the man telephoned to report the onset of labor. He was breathless and so confused that his wife had to take over to receive final instructions. The obstetrician arrived at the hospital about an hour before the couple, who had lost their way. At the reception desk, the woman took care of all the admission details. Everyone was too busy to notice that the man was becoming paler and paler and sweating profusely. By the time the expectant mother was ready to receive her spouse in the labor room, an intern had to be called to revive him.

How do expectant couples themselves feel about the husband's presence in the labor room? The differences of opinion are significant. Most couples who have had no preparation-for-labor course agree that the husband should stay out. The women are afraid they will make fools of themselves, that they will be unattractive during labor, that they will be more nervous with the husband than without him. The men muster a variety of reasons to convince themselves and their wives that an expectant father's place is anywhere except the labor room. One husband went so far as to persuade his personal physician to sign a statement to the effect that his health was so precarious that he should not be allowed in the labor room.

The majority of couples who have had a preparation-for-labor course but who have not yet had their babies are perfectly willing to try the experiment. Most couples who have once had a baby with the father in the labor room are enthusiastic about it. In a survey of such couples at one of the country's largest maternity hospitals only one father in twenty-five said he would not do the same thing with the next baby. All the others said that they had been of some help, had profited from the experience, and felt closer to their wives and children as a result of it. While the mothers were not quite as close to unanimity, the majority felt that their husband's presence in the labor room had been most helpful and hoped that with their next babies the father would again be with them during the first stage of childbirth. The few dissenters said that the facilities were inadequate, that men could not take the strain, that they preferred to be alone when they were under stress.

The perceptive physician will, of course, be wary of the motives of the rare wife who wants her husband to be with her for reasons that are less than noble. One woman insisted that her husband be present during the first stage of labor and was disappointed that hospital rules forbade him to witness the actual delivery. She said her pains were unbearable and she constantly demanded that he apply ice packs to her head, rub her back and legs, "do something." She would squeeze his hand and arm until he was in pain. As soon as he left the room—always against her wishes—she would become calm. When questioned about this, the woman replied that she wanted her husband to suffer more than she did, that she was "teaching him a lesson" and showing him that she was "suffering for him and because of him." This performance was repeated during three successive labors despite her obstetrician's opposition.

How to Decide

If your hospital has individual labor rooms and the larger nursing staff that enable you to be with your wife during labor, you must decide together whether to take advantage of it. Here are a few questions that may help both of you decide. How have you reacted in the past when your wife has been under stress or in pain? When one of you is worried about an important problem, does that one seek advice and support from the other or go to friends and relatives? Most important, do both of you really want you to be in the labor room, or are you only yielding to some kind of pressure?

Your presence in the delivery room is an altogether different matter. The vast majority of hospitals in this country don't admit the husband to the actual delivery. There are a number of practical reasons for this rule. All who enter the delivery room must be properly dressed and carefully instructed in the maintenance of strict asepsis. You would have to wear a sterile "scrub suit," gown, and shoes. In a hospital delivering fifteen to twenty babies a day, the necessary supervision would require much time. There may be very little time immediately before a delivery—if labor is progressing rapidly, things sometimes become hectic. Each person in the delivery room is a member of a well-trained and highly coordinated team and must peform his job quickly and efficiently. In a misguided attempt to be helpful, you might get in the way at a crucial moment. If, for example, you were inadvertently to touch the clothing of a sterilely clad nurse or doctor, that person would have to take time out to change.

Nevertheless, times are changing, and an increasing number of hospitals do permit fathers in the delivery room. If you have taken a course with your wife and have been instructed what to do, if facilities are available, and if you have discussed it with your doctor, being present at the actual birth of your child can be a memorable and thrilling experience. In one large hospital the number of fathers present in the delivery room has increased from less than 1 percent five years ago to over 20 percent at this time. If you are allowed in the delivery room, your place is next to your wife at the head of the table so that she can talk to you and you can help her during the actual delivery. You should not wander around the delivery room or try to look over the doctor's shoulder unless you are specifically asked to do so.

CHAPTER 15

The Long Wait Downstairs

All expectant fathers must be prepared to endure long and usually lonely periods of waiting. Even if you plan to be with your wife during her labor, you will be forced to wait, both before you are admitted to the labor room and after she has been taken to the delivery room. If you are not going to be in the labor room, you won't see your wife at all from the time you kiss her as she is escorted into the elevator until perhaps hours later—especially if this is a first baby—when you are finally permitted to visit her briefly after the child has been born and she has returned to her room. There are many things to be done, and some of them require privacy.

As soon as your wife gets to the labor room, she will be helped into a hospital gown and possibly be examined by the house doctor, who will communicate and report his findings to your own doctor. You may think that this young physician ought to take the time to tell you what is happening, but remember that he is very busy, that there may also be other women in labor and therefore other expectant fathers, and that his first responsibility is to your wife and not to you. Don't try to waylay him in the corridors—he won't answer your questions because this is not his proper role. Your own doctor, after he has arrived and made his own examination, will speak to you. Be available. If you must get a drink, get it in a nearby bar and leave the telephone number with the hospital clerk or registrar.

Don't be like the husband who expected to join his wife in the labor room as soon as she was admitted. Asked to wait in the lobby, he drove the entire staff to distraction by collaring everyone who crossed his path, constantly bothering the switchboard operator to call the labor floor, and finally sneaking up the stairs to find out for himself what was going on. By the time he was permitted to enter the labor room, he was so nervous and exhausted that he changed his mind about being with his wife—for which the obstetrician was grateful.

While hospital routines vary, and while the circumstances in an individual case may require modifications, most women are given an enema, a shower, and a vaginal "prep" after their initial examination. The first of these procedures is designed to empty the lower bowel. The second two procedures are designed to render the skin as free from bacterial contamination as possible. Some of these procedures may be unpleasant and even uncomfortable, and require the utmost privacy of nurse and patient. You must realize that they are time-consuming and, if there are other women who are closer to delivery than your wife, she may have to wait her turn.

The initial waiting period may seem unduly long to you, but it is important, both for your own well-being and that of your wife, that you remain calm. The best way to do this is to keep busy. Resist the temptation to seek comfort from your relatives, especially from your wife's relatives. If you telephone them now, you won't be able to give them a single bit of useful information. Instead, you are more likely to worry them, and they in turn will add to your anxiety. Some may even insist on joining you in your vigil. One large hospital was recently invaded by an entire tribe of Gypsies when an expectant father called his mother-in-law to tell her that her daughter was in labor. In good Gypsy tradition of family loyalty and unity, the clan, including distant cousins, children, and nursing infants, arrived. They set up camp in the lobby, and although the staff appreciated the humor of the situation (as well as the food that poured out of baskets, valises, and paper bags), they were not amused by the interference with their duties nor by the necessity of finally having the noisy horde gently but firmly ejected.

Passing the Time

Expectant fathers do all sorts of things to pass the time. Some just sit and stare. Others pace nervously to and fro, lighting cigarette after cigarette but smoking few. Still others commiserate with their fellows in the waiting room, hoping to find at least one with enough prior experience and patience to answer questions intelligently. The best thing to do is to be prepared. Bring along a book, a magazine, a batch of crossword puzzles, or a solitary game. If you like to listen to the radio, don't depend on finding one in working order in the waiting room; your pocket-size transistor will be more dependable and, if you use the earpiece, less likely to annoy any non-music-loving neighbors. If you are a teacher, a lawyer, a writer, or engaged in any other occupation requiring paper work, bring some of it along. An accountant, for example, entertained himself by determining exactly how much tax money would be saved over the years as a result of the new dependency claim that was on the way. This is a good opportunity, too, to prepare the list of telephone numbers that you will need as soon as the good news finally comes. Even if you have made such a list in advance, the act of poring over your address book and all available directories will remind you of many long-lost friends and will revive many fond memories.

There are a few things you should not do. One drink is perfectly permissible and may even be advisable, but wait until later to stand treat around the bar. Don't try to unwind by taking a long drive. In the first place, you should be within easy call of the hospital, and the registrar should know your whereabouts. In the second place, your emotional state is not likely to make you the safest driver on the road. Above all, don't follow the example of the expectant father who ate so much that by the time his baby arrived, he had developed a bellyache so severe he could not fully appreciate the joyful event.

The baby will come when it's ready, and there is nothing you can do to hasten it. Sometimes the switchboard operator will be entrusted with delivering the good news, sometimes a nurse from the delivery floor. Many obstetricians prefer to see the new father personally, even if he has already been informed. They feel that they can provide the most accurate information and the greatest degree of assurance. You will understand that the doctor cannot dash down to see you the moment the baby is born. He still has many essential things to do for your wife and for the infant before he can leave them. Until he has fulfilled these responsibilities, he does not have the time to reassure you that everything has gone well.

As a matter of fact, it is a good idea to wait for the doctor, even if you have already heard the good news from someone else, for mistakes will happen. In one case, there were four expectant fathers in the waiting room. The delivery floor called down to tell the two men whose wives had arrived earliest that their babies had been born. When the telephone rang the next time, the third man, who assumed that babies were born in the order of their mother's arrival, answered the call and was told that he had a seven-pound daughter. He called all his relatives and friends and dashed out to buy a bouquet of pink roses for his wife. When he returned, his doctor, who had been searching for him, shook his hand and congratulated him on being the father of twin boys.

CHAPTER 16

Safeguarding the Baby during Labor

It has been said that the baby's descent through the birth canal during labor represents the greatest risk to which he will be exposed from the time of his conception onward. His entry into the outside world may be compared to the astronauts' reentry into the earth's atmosphere from outer space. This statement sounds more ominous than it really is, for one of the marvels of the birth of a child is the remarkable adaptation from intrauterine to extrauterine life. That the infant, when delivered, will give a lusty cry has come to be taken for granted—and this is in fact what happens in the great majority of cases.

To avoid any complications, special methods of monitoring the fetus in labor have recently been developed. The traditional and most widely used method to check the fetus during labor is the stethoscope by which the doctor or nurse listens to the fetal heartbeat between contractions. If no problems arise, this is an excellent procedure and suffices in most cases. However, since listening with a stethoscope cannot be continuous and is dependent upon human rather than machine counting, early signs of fetal distress may be missed.

Fetal Scalp Blood Sampling

One of the most accurate methods of evaluating the condition of the baby in labor was developed by Erich Saling of Germany.

It is called fetal scalp blood sampling. A drop of blood from the fetal scalp is tested by biochemical methods to determine the oxygen exchange between baby and mother. If repeated examinations reveal a disturbance in the fetal acid-base equilibrium, immediate delivery by forceps or by Caesarean section can be performed thereby preventing severe damage to the baby or even stillbirth. This test has also been useful in preventing operative interference when the stethoscope indicates alteration in the fetal heart rate. If repeated sampling of fetal scalp blood shows no disturbance in the acid-base equilibrium, rapid delivery is not necessary and labor is permitted to continue.

Electronic Fetal Monitor

A new technique of electronic fetal monitoring, which involves simultaneously recording the fetal heartbeat and the mother's uterine contractions during labor, has been introduced in some hospitals. The equipment is compact, portable, and simple to use. An electrode is attached to the baby's head and a thin Teflon tube inserted into the mother's uterus. The fetal electrocardiograph is shown on an oscilloscope and the fetal heart rate appears simultaneously on an adjacent meter. The mother's uterine contractions are traced on a chart. A beep sounds with each beat of the baby's heart, allowing the doctor or nurse to leave the room and still be aware of the baby's condition.

Fetal monitoring is of great value in the management of high-risk pregnancies involving such conditions as toxemia, chronic hypertension, diabetes, Rh sensitization, premature rupture of the membranes, and post-date pregnancies, as well as in induced labor. Where medication is used to increase uterine contractions, electronic fetal monitoring is particularly helpful. By continuously monitoring the baby's heart rate and the mother's uterine contractions, the exact level of safety can be determined. Continuous monitoring also allows the doctor to recognize difficulties as soon as they arise, institute corrective measures, and thus prevent damage to the baby.

The main drawback to this type of equipment is its cost. Although fetal monitoring is not yet available in all hospitals, such techniques are becoming increasingly popular. Should it be necessary to use this equipment on your wife and baby during labor, you can be assured that these extra precautions are being taken for their welfare. Since you have read this description of the electronic fetal monitor, you will be able to explain what is happening to your wife to lessen her apprehension.

Echo-Tone Doppler

Another simple method of monitoring the baby's heart rate is with an Echo-Tone Doppler ultrasonic instrument. This magnifies the heartbeat so it can be heard by means of a hand probe or with a flat probe that can be attached to the abdomen and left in place. To hear this loud heartbeat is most comforting to your wife, to you, and to the attendants.

CHAPTER 17

The Birth of Your Child

Labor, or the process of giving birth to a baby, is just what the term implies—hard work. The attitudes that you both have developed throughout marriage and the pregnancy, and especially the frame of mind in which both of you approach the present situation, can help to determine whether your wife's labor will be difficult or easy. A woman who looks forward to motherhood and is encouraged by a husband equally eager about fatherhood is likely to have a relatively pleasant labor and delivery. The fear and anxiety that contribute to pain are almost completely dispelled by anticipation of the joys to come. On the other hand, if the fearful and resentful husband consciously or unconsciously communicates his feelings to his wife, her own anxiety is apt to be intensified. She could have an unpleasant labor and delivery that might affect your whole marriage. This is the time for you to be controlled without being tense, to be cheerful and reassuring, to be tender and considerate. Try to remember how you felt while you were performing the hardest physical and psychological task that you ever attempted in your life. Try to remember just how someone helped you and how someone less sensitive may have hindered you. Act accordingly!

The First Stage of Labor

Almost every husband spends the earlier portion of the first stage of labor with his wife, for it usually takes place at home and en route to the hospital. If you are going to remain with your wife during any part of the later stages, you will want to help—and you can. If not, you will still want to know what is going on.

During the first stage of labor, which is also the longest, especially with a first child, the cervix, or tip of the womb, must be sufficiently stretched to permit the baby to emerge. This process of dilatation takes place by means of uterine contractions over which your wife has no control. The muscular walls of the womb exert pressure on the fetus, either directly or via the bag of waters while it is still intact. These waves of pressure force the baby farther and farther down the womb, causing the cervix to stretch from its original closed state to a width of about four inches. It is as if you were to use your hands to force a ball down through a resilient tube with an elastic opening. As the ball is forced lower and lower in the tube, the opening stretches until it becomes large enough to permit the ball to drop out. At first these uterine contractions come at intervals of about fifteen minutes, and the pain which may accompany each one is comparatively mild. Gradually they come more often and with greater intensity until, toward the end of the first stage of labor, they recur every four or five minutes.

It is most important that your wife avoid consciously bearing down during contractions and that she relax between them. Active participation at this stage and excess tension at any stage will increase pain and lengthen labor. If you took one of the preparation-for-labor courses, you can help by applying some of the specific physical and psychological measures that you learned in these classes, and especially by reassuring your wife and reminding her that every uterine effort is bringing the baby closer and closer. Since she will be reasonably comfortable and alert between contractions, she can be helped to relax by some sort of amusement or diversion. If you are present, you can certainly help. Some wives just want to talk. Try to steer the conversation toward light topics, but avoid humor that just isn't funny and especially jokes that poke fun at the very experience through which your wife is going—she simply won't appreciate them. Many women enjoy having their husbands read to them, or playing cards or such games as anagrams. One obstetrician enjoys telling about a patient who became so engrossed in a game of cards she and her husband were playing, and at which she was winning, that she didn't realize that she was almost ready for delivery. Of course, this woman had a very pleasant labor and almost no pain. She insisted later that her only memories concerned the mistakes she had made which prevented her winning even more money from her husband.

At the Hospital

You will, of course, guard against getting in the way, offering medical advice, or interfering in any way with the doctor or his assistants. When you are asked to leave the room briefly, and this will happen frequently, do so promptly. The doctor may want to examine your wife or perform some procedure, and privacy is essential. Remember that you chose your doctor because you had a great deal of confidence in him. Don't lose that confidence now.

Here is an example of the worst kind of interference. Convinced of the advantages of "natural" childbirth by some of his male friends, a man insisted that his wife accept this well-established but not always feasible method. The doctor was a believer in natural childbirth, but warned them that it was not always practicable. As matters turned out, the woman went into an unusually long and difficult labor. Instead of comforting his wife and supporting the doctor in his recommendation that she accept an analgesic, the husband berated her, telling her that she was a disappointment and that her cowardliness was endangering his baby. To fulfill his responsibility to the patient, the obstetrician finally forced the husband to leave the labor room so that the wife could calm down and respond to analgesia. When it was found that the baby would have to be delivered by Caesarean section, the husband refused to sign the necessary permission form. The obstetrician had no choice but to perform the operation without the consent of the husband in order to save the lives of the wife and the baby. A male infant weighing over ten pounds was delivered at operation, and both mother and baby were fine. To this day, the physician wonders what inner need the husband had that made him insist that his wife not receive any relief from pain, and what effect this experience had on mother, father, and child.

The Second Stage of Labor

The second stage of labor, which is much shorter than the first —sometimes lasting only a few minutes with later children—starts after the cervix has been fully dilated and ends with the delivery of the child. While the contractions of the first stage serve principally to stretch the opening of the womb, those of the second operate mainly to expel the fetus. They come at shorter intervals and are usually accompanied by less pain, which can be eased by the same techniques that were used earlier.

Depending on the wishes of you, your wife, and your physician, on hospital policy, and on whether this is a first or later baby, you may or may not be present during the phase of this stage that takes place in the labor room. If you are, you can help by encouraging your wife to bear down actively with each contraction and to relax and breathe deeply between them. By bearing down with each contraction, the woman assists the muscles of the uterus in their task of expelling the baby into the outer world. During this second stage, there will be a doctor or a nurse in the room, or one of them will be coming in very often, and as soon as the top of the infant's head becomes visible in the vagina, your wife will be taken to the delivery room, and you will be asked to leave.

While you are pacing the floor, talking with other expectant fathers or otherwise trying to occupy the time, your wife will be in the hands of a carefully trained and highly coordinated delivery room team prepared to cope with any situation. There will be nurses to take care of her and the baby after it is born. An anesthetist will be ready to administer some pain-relieving agent should this become necessary. And, of course, there will be the obstetrician and at least one physician assistant to perform the actual delivery. The room itself will be equipped with the most modern and reliable equipment, ready to be put into action as soon as it is needed. Usually, of course, the delivery is completely normal and no emergency arises. As the baby descends into the vagina, the doctor will probably perform an episiotomy, which is a small and readily repaired incision designed to avoid tearing of the delicate tissues of the vagina. If there is the slightest trouble, he will use techniques involving forceps or other special instruments, but these procedures pose almost no threat to mother or baby. Even the ancient operation of Caesarean section is now one of the safest of all surgical procedures and, contrary to an old tradition, does not affect a woman's ability to have more children.

As soon as the infant is born, the doctor will make sure that it is breathing properly and give it to a nurse who will place in each eye a drop of solution or an antibotic ointment that prevents blindness from infection. She will wash the child, wrap it in warm, soft blankets, and take it to the nursery. At the same time, the obstetrician will again have turned his attention to your wife for the brief third stage of labor which is the delivery of the after-birth or placenta. Soon after, she will be lying comfortably in her room, washed, combed, ready to greet you with that mysterious and special smile that appears only on the face of a woman who has just performed the age-old task of bearing a child.

The First Look

Some hospitals may allow you to see your baby before you are permitted to see your wife. Face the facts. Newborn infants are seldom very beautiful except to their mothers. They are likely to have large heads which may appear lopsided; their hair, if any, is messy, and their eyes stare blankly and unsteadily at nothing. If they do respond to your greeting through the nursery window, the response will probably take the form of a violent howl. But take heart. Within a day or so, your baby will be the most beautiful ever born, at least to you.

If you are disappointed, don't let it show when you see your wife at last. Don't even start by talking about the baby. First ask about her. She has undergone an intense and stressful experience and, though she is well and proud, needs your love and reassurance. Tell her that she looks more beautiful than ever, for she probably does, and don't shock and frighten her by letting her see you haggard and disheveled. Make every effort to be enthusiastic about the baby even if it does resemble her family instead of yours. If you pull any boners at this stage, your wife will never forget— even if she eventually does forgive them. This is a good time, too, to discuss visiting. Assure her that you will visit her whenever possible, but call her attention to any unavoidable commitments that may keep you away. If she is expecting you and you don't show up or call to say you can't make it, she will be justifiably disappointed and angry. If she knows of your plans, she may still be disappointed, but she is likely to be understanding. Ask whether she'd like you to bring anything when you visit, or whether you can do any errands for her. On subsequent visits, bring a surprise gift just for her—perhaps a bauble that she has always fancied, or, if you can afford it, a piece of jewelry that she will afterwards always associate with this happy period of her life. Small, familiar objects from home will help to soften the institutional atmosphere of a hospital room—a favorite picture, a trinket that may have deep meaning to both of you. This may also be the time to discuss circumcision. This minor procedure is now almost universally practiced and is usually performed in the hospital by a doctor. If ritual circumcision is required, make the necessary arrangements through your wife's obstetrician. Finally, leave promptly so that your wife can get some much-needed sleep, and go to the nearest telephone booth to notify grandparents, relatives, and friends.

You also need some warning about what you can expect to find on later visits. If your wife is like most women, her initial elation will give way, in a day or two, to a period of depression. This is brought about by the perfectly natural reaction to a physically and emotionally exhausting experience, by some degree of discomfort and pain caused by the procedures she has undergone, by concern about whether she will make a good mother and be able to handle all the difficulties involved in raising a child, and by many other physical and emotional factors. Such a depression is absolutely normal and almost invariably temporary. She will probably feel all right in a day or two, and you should tell her so, doubling the reassurance that her doctor will also give her. You can also help by being with her as often as possible, by shielding her from annoying visitors, and by starting to plan with her for your new life together with a baby. If she is convinced of your love for her and the child, this period of depression will not only pass but will lead to a profound understanding between you and to a feeling of common serenity that will help both of you to be a happier married couple and better parents.

CHAPTER 18

Bringing Baby Home

Preparation for bringing the baby home should begin long before the actual day of the big event. If there are older children, they should have been prepared for the newcomer weeks or even months in advance. Regardless of their ages, the new child represents a threat to them, or at least serious competition. No matter how carefully and tactfully they have been told that there is going to be a new sister or brother, no matter how completely and happily they seem to have accepted the fact, there is bound to be some jealousy. This may manifest itself in a variety of ways and is likely to be precipitated by the shock of the mother's departure for the hospital and by her absence for many days.

Older Children

One three-year-old girl had known almost from the beginning that her mother was pregnant. She seemed pleased at the prospect of a new baby in the family and was deeply interested in everything that was happening over the nine months. When she was awakened one night, told that the baby was on its way, and bundled off to an aunt's house according to advance plan, she appeared to be delighted. However, on his first visit to the girl after the birth of a new daughter, the father realized something was wrong. The little girl clung to him throughout his stay, and though she did not try to keep him from leaving, he saw her standing at a window, watching him sadly as he drove away. He decided to take the rest of the week off from work and take care

101

of the child himself in their own home. Thereafter, things seemed perfectly fine until the day before his wife and new baby were due to return from the hospital. That afternoon, he noticed that his daughter seemed lethargic and warm. When he took her temperature, he found that she had a fever and called the doctor. Throughout the night the little girl tossed and turned in her bed and the father could feel the heat radiating from her body. He asked a friend to drive his wife and the new baby home from the hospital while he remained at home to nurse the sick child. When his wife came home and embraced her older daughter, the child recovered with dramatic suddenness.

Before the new baby is born, you and your wife will share the responsibility for preparing the older children. In every possible way, show them that they are still loved and that nothing can interfere with this love. If a room or a crib must be given up to the newcomer, this should be done well in advance so that the necessary physical and emotional adjustments can be made. New toys and clothes, a special treat, even a little excess pampering, will help.

Once your wife goes to the hospital you must play the major role in seeing to it that the older children are not neglected or hurt, because she will have to devote most of her time, at least for a few weeks, to the baby. Plan to spend more time at home than you usually do. If the older children seem more annoying and difficult than ever, don't lose your patience; remember that they are having their own problems. Occasionally, they may revert to infantile behavior. Some will insist on being fed, or even on taking the bottle or the breast when they observe the baby enjoying these privileges. Others will have temper tantrums and crying fits. A few may even go back to bed-wetting when they notice that this gets attention. Whenever possible, permit the older child to satisfy these infantile desires—they will soon disappear. Don't scold or punish, for this does no good and will probably make matters worse.

More serious, and more difficult to handle, are the occasional attempts to harm the baby. These are overt reflections of the hidden wish of every human being, no matter what age, to hurt a rival. Many child psychiatrists feel that it is much healthier for such behavior to come out into the open than to fester within.

The best method of managing this situation, as well as less serious ones, is to show, by deeds more than by words, that you really love the older child as much as the younger. Another device is to encourage the older child to help with the baby and to accept certain simple responsibilities for its welfare. This will foster a feeling of big brotherhood or sisterhood and help lay the foundation for an excellent relationship among all the children in the family throughout their lives.

Shopping for Baby

There are many things you can do for the new baby and for your wife during the intervals between your visits to the hospital. No doubt your wife has already bought most of the layette. However, she probably left a few items for you, chiefly those that would have to be either pink or blue. Don't let a mother-in-law or friend deprive you of the fun of shopping for these yourself. The salespeople in department stores and infant specialty shops are glad to help new fathers make practical selections. But avoid being too practical. Cater to the new baby—and to your own desire for being a part of the whole sequence of blessed events—by splurging on that supersoft (and superexpensive) thingamajig they wrap babies in during the winter. If that high-priced, frilly carriage robe appeals to you, buy it. When funds run low, you can cut down on lunches for a few months, and such a deprivation will be good for your body as well as your soul.

Be a wastrel, too, when you make that first trip to the toy store. No doubt you'll have as much fun shopping for toys as the baby will have playing with them, but try to remember that your child must be considered first. A later chapter will go into some detail about the selection of toys during the first year, but since you probably won't be able to resist the temptation of buying some before the baby is home, you may need a few immediate pointers.

Even the youngest infant will love the sound of a small bell or a muffled rattle. A simple mobile suspended from a string over the crib or across its rails will catch the baby's eyes as soon as they are able to focus. Later, when the child is able to clutch and strike, these colorful and musical gadgets will provide limitless amusement. And make sure that these first toys are so sturdy and so beautiful that they can become mementos or even heirlooms.

You should be much more practical when it comes to buying furniture and other "hard" equipment. Your local lumber dealer will advise you on how to build some of these items yourself and how to make others by reconstructing ordinary household objects. The basic requirement is a place for the baby to sleep. A regulation-size crib is not very convenient during the first few weeks. The infant seems lost in it, the rails get in your wife's way, and the bars, even when they are padded or otherwise protected, always seem so spaced and placed that they trap a baby's head, arms, or legs. If you can't buy or borrow a bassinet, improvise with a wash basket, a drawer, or even a sturdy carton. Let your imagination run wild in decorating the makeshift, but make sure it is practical. Pad the sides and keep it on a large bed or couch so that if it does overturn, no harm will be done. Don't use a pillow for a mattress—it isn't firm or flat enough, and an infant can suffocate in it. Instead, fold an old blanket so that it fits the bassinet smoothly and snugly, and cover it with some moisture-proof material such as rubber, heavy plastic, or oilcloth. If you simply cannot wait for your wife to help in the selection of a full-size crib for later use, get one that is large enough so that the baby will be able to use it for about three years. Be certain that the mattress is firm and that there is a pad or some other protective device for the bars.

You and your wife have probably already decided where the new baby will sleep. Most mothers want the infant in the bedroom with them for at least a few weeks. If the baby must share your bedroom beyond this time, you may want to use shoulder-high screens or rearrange the bookcases, dressers, or other furniture to give you some privacy. Later, you will want to make more permanent arrangements if your apartment or house does not have a child's room.

The purchase of such major objects as a carriage, a chest, a high chair, and a playpen can and should await the return of your wife, and you ought to convince even doting grandparents and maiden aunts of this. But you should take care of such immediately necessary things as a bathtub and dressing table. The combination known as a bathinette is popular, but substitutes can be improvised. The important things to consider are safety and convenience.

Therefore, both the bathtub and the table should be sturdy and well balanced, light enough so that your wife can move them about easily, and high enough so that she won't strain her back bending over them. You should also make a trip to the drug store. The baby's doctor will advise you about soap, baby oil, cotton balls, bottles, nipples, formula-making equipment, and the innumerable other items that will be needed as soon as the baby comes home. Make sure to arrange for diaper delivery if you are going to use this convenient service, or, if you are not, stock up on disposable diapers or arrange some method of storing and washing soiled diapers. Finally, be certain to notify the practical nurse or other helper for whom previous arrangements have been made of the time and day of arrival of mother and child.

The Big Day

On the big day itself, do your very best to be free of all other responsibilities. Some men arrange to take all or part of their vacations at this time, and this is an especially good idea if you haven't been able to provide some sort of help for your wife. Before you leave for the hospital, take a careful look around the house. Make sure that it is neat and clean, and be particularly wary of those small details that always annoy your wife if they are done or undone, as the case may be. Have the baby's bassinet prepared and your wife's bed made. See to it that there is a snack or a meal in the refrigerator, or arrange to have one delivered at the proper time. Fill all the vases with fresh flowers if your budget allows.

Once again, be sure that you get to the hospital on time. Your wife will probably be pacing up and down, anxious to go home, and any delay you cause will be singularly unappreciated. If you are driving, arrange to have a third person with you to help with the baby, but tactfully suggest that any assistance be withheld until your wife specifically requests it. Be even more forceful in insisting on your right to enter your wife's room alone—this is a moment not to be shared with anyone else. Arrive at the hospital early enough so that the payment of bills and the completion of discharge papers and other required forms will not delay your wife's departure. Hospital officials will then help you claim your wife and child and will assist them into the waiting automobile. When that door closes and the nurse or the attendant waves good-bye, the responsibility for your family is yours alone. Make sure that everyone is safely and comfortably settled, and do drive home carefully—there are three of you to worry about now.

CHAPTER 19

Life with a New Baby— and a New Mother

Your life changed greatly when you became a husband, but the change is likely to be even more drastic when you become a father. This is not to say that either change is for the worse—indeed, they are usually for the better. However, it is impossible to deny the difficulties. And the most crucial and trying period in adjusting to fatherhood is the first six weeks or so after the new baby comes home with the new mother.

In the discharge room of a large New York maternity hospital, a sign on the wall reads: "Nobody is born a parent. Everyone learns to be a parent as a result of his own life experience, the information he has accumulated, the facts he has observed and the actual living with and caring for a child." While it is possible that the deep biological tie a mother has to her child during the nine months of pregnancy is responsible for something called "mother's instinct," there is no corresponding father's instinct. The child's link to the father begins the day of the child's birth and is a social one. As the first representative of the outside world, your impact is great, and it can become a strong bond with your child or an insignificant one.

You can share actively in the care of your infant—carry him in your arms, play with him, bathe him, rush home from work to be with him and strengthen the bond. Whether you spend many hours with your child or see him seldom, your relationship with him influences his future development. Playing with father can be unpredictable—pleasant, startling, frightening. You can instill a sense of triumph, strength, independence just because you seem so big. The little child lifted to your shoulder looks out at the world and can see more than taller children, can feel himself expand—grow larger. Children all over the world argue as to whose father is taller, stronger, smarter. Children can take their failures to their mothers where they will regain composure, but they may hesitate to tell their fathers the "bad" things that happened to them. Perhaps some fathers reprimand too severely.

You will have to learn to be a good father, and you will also have to learn to be a good husband to the woman who is no longer merely your wife but the mother of your child.

Learning to Be a Father

Like all learning, this takes some patience and study and may be accompanied by occasional failures and frustrations; but like all learning, it, too, will provide tremendous satisfactions and rewards. In learning how to cope with your child, you will grow and develop as a father and as a more stable and less self-centered human being, better able than ever before to manage the trials of life and living.

Your new experience may even help you with your job. One high-school principal states quite frankly that he much prefers to hire teachers who are parents, not only because of their deeper understanding of and sympathy with children, but because they have learned practical ways of handling teenagers and their problems.

But these are only the bonuses of fatherhood. Your primary problem is to become a good father and husband, and your greatest joy will come through mastering this double skill. Since all the theory in the world will not help unless you put it into actual practice, finish all the books you have been reading, including this one, and get to know your baby.

At first, there is not much to know. The infant spends most of its time sleeping—if you are lucky—and its few waking hours feeding. But even during this comparatively quiescent stage of existence, you can participate in doing things for the baby, and in so doing you can gain some satisfaction from the knowledge that you are contributing to the growth and development of your child as well as helping your wife. At the very least, you can take pictures—you will regret it if you don't. In focusing your camera on the baby, you will notice cute and unusual traits that give it a distinctive personality. One father constantly boasted to his commuting companions about the outlandish positions his son assumed during sleep. Another countered that he would stack his daughter's snores and wheezes against those of any other child in the community, both in volume and in variety of sounds. A third stopped all further conversation when he challenged any father on the train to produce an infant with as large a bladder capacity as his offspring's. Silly talk for men? Certainly not! Wonderful talk, for it reflects love and attention and concern, some of the most important qualities of fatherhood.

But don't be merely an observer, a photographer and a boaster. Ask your wife to teach you how to perform the innumerable chores required in the care of an infant. Then practice them carefully under her supervision until both of you are satisfied that you can do them without harming the baby, the household effects, or yourself. Finally, insist that she go to a movie or visit with friends while you take complete charge for an entire evening. It will be a revelation—and good for you.

First, you will have to bathe the baby. As your wife taught you, test the temperature of the water with your elbow; if you prefer to be scientific, check with a thermometer. Then remove the diaper without plastering baby, table, walls, and yourself with a sticky mess. Your next job is to carry the diaper, along with the baby (unless you can put him in a secure place), into the bathroom. There you can rinse the diaper in the toilet bowl before disposing of it in the diaper can. When you lose the diaper down the drain, you will recall, and perhaps regret, the temper you flew into the last time your wife told you she had to call the plumber.

Now comes the most ticklish part—and the most fun. Having spent so many months floating in the amniotic fluid, the infant is absolutely comfortable and relaxed in a warm bath. It is here that babies are most likely to show the beginnings of individuality and personality. The cooing, stretching, and thrashing of arms and legs with resultant splashing of water are really amusing. In your enthusiasm, however, don't drop the baby. Support the back and head at all times and apply the washcloth gently. Be gentle when you are patting the skin dry, cleaning out crevices and folds with cotton balls, anointing with oil or dusting with powder. During the last procedure, incidentally, be careful not to get any powder near the infant's eyes, nose, or mouth.

Now take a little time out to play with your child. If you place a finger firmly against the palm, the little hand will clutch you firmly. If you lift the baby gently into the air, he will arch his back, stretch, wave his limbs, and gurgle with delight. Help the baby to exercise his arms and legs. They will start to become strong and both you and the baby will have a grand time. Buy a tiny flashlight and watch how the eyes will begin to focus and follow the beam. During this and other play periods, do whatever seems natural and whatever the baby appears to enjoy. But don't try to roughhouse until the child is much older. Many infants have ended up with twisted backs and necks as a result of too vigorous tossing-and-throwing games.

While the bottle is warming, proceed with diapering and dressing, and then hold the baby gently and quietly in your arms so that he can relax and calm down before feeding. Even if you don't have much of a voice, babies will enjoy hearing you sing at this time, and even if you sound perfectly silly to yourself, your youngster will love to hear you talk. Remember to test a drop of milk on the inside of your wrist to be sure it's not too hot.

You will find that getting a squirming infant to take the nipple and consume the contents of a bottle without spraying you and the surrounding territory with tepid milk is a challenge worthy of your masculinity. If that task is not sufficiently difficult to satisfy your male ego, just try holding a child over your shoulder and "burping" or "bubbling" it without having the whole meal come up on your shirt. (It's a good idea to put a clean diaper on your shoulder just in case.) Go through this ritual while observing your child in a mirror. Seldom will you see anything as heartwarming as the look of blissful satisfaction that comes over a baby's face when the gas is finally expelled. Incidentally, you may now see a smile, or the semblance of a smile, for the first time.

After the baby has been fed, re-diapered, and put to sleep, if you have any remaining energy and want to gain an even deeper in-

sight into the problems your wife faces every day, you might prepare the formula and sterile drinking water for the next day. Many
men enjoy this job and insist on doing it for their wives. One
wife, however, began to wonder why it took her husband such a
long time to get the task done. She finally discovered that he was
not only boiling and re-boiling the milk and the water, but then
carefully passing them through a porcelain filter he had bought in
a laboratory supply house. He was trying to remove the dead
germs. It took a serious lecture by the doctor to convince this
overconcerned father that dead germs were absolutely harmless.

Excessive concern with the baby's welfare and development may,
indeed, cause more problems for you, your wife, and the child
than lack of concern. Most of these unnecessary worries are the
result of ignorance or misinformation, and a careful reading of one
of the books devoted to child-rearing listed in Appendix III will
spare all of you much anxiety.

The four areas that seem to bother parents most frequently are
eating, sleeping, crying, and bowel movements. Just remember
that most infants instinctively do what is best for them and avoid
doing what will harm them. There is no rule that an infant must
consume a specified amount at each feeding. Nor must an infant
sleep for a required number of hours each day; if a baby prefers
to stare at the walls or to make strange noises at observers, that is
perfectly all right. Crying should not cause alarm. While it is true
that a few minutes of hard crying will not harm the baby, crying
for a long period will do him no good and may make him fearful
and fretful. Your child will usually cry less if you respond promptly
to his signals. Don't be afraid of spoiling him. When you get to
know your baby, you will soon be able to distinguish among his
cries and take appropriate action. Finally, don't worry about bowel
movements and, of course, save toilet training for much later. If
you have any questions about any of these matters or about other
health problems, be sure to get the answers from a doctor and not
from well-meaning friends or grandparents.

Grandparents

Dealing with grandparents, especially during the first few weeks, is a problem unto itself, particularly if your baby is a first grandchild. Most grandparents want to see and love their grandchildren and are anxious to do things for them, and you should deprive neither them nor the infant of these pleasures. There isn't anything wrong in letting them kiss the baby; their germs are no more virulent than yours. However, you and your wife must remember that you are the child's parents, and that the responsibility for its rearing and welfare is yours alone. Listen to the grandparents' advice and consider their suggestions, but make all final decisions yourselves. Otherwise many tensions are likely to arise, and these will affect the entire family, including the baby.

A few years ago, John Canaday, art critic of *The New York Times,* offered some advice to grandparents from his experience as a four-year-old grandfather. First, the grandparent should begin by going overboard immediately and referring to the child as "an angel of delight." Second, grandparents must follow the dictum "Mother and Daddy are always right." Mr. Canaday does not believe that the grandparent should join with the grandchild against the common enemy, the parent. Grandparents should stay out of such responsible decisions as whether extra cookie rations should be issued, whether naps are necessary at certain hours, and whether ball playing should be permitted in the living room. The grandparent's total involvement in parent-child conflicts should be to make available a comforting lap for either grandchild or parent. The total vocabulary in this time of crisis should be limited to "There, there." The grandparent cannot assume the role of a referee, a ringsider, or a participant. He is something special, "a combination of parent, playmate and Santa Claus."

The cliché concerning grandparenthood, "You have all the pleasures with none of the responsibility," is untrue on both scores, Mr. Canaday says. Grandparents do not have all the pleasure; they had it when they were parents, and half the time they hated it. The grandparent has the negative responsibility of keeping hands off, except when he is asked officially for help, which usually is in the form of an SOS. Between emergencies, the grandparent is a has-been who enjoys a kind of biologically reflected glory.

Older Children

In your enthusiasm about the new member of the family, be sure not to forget that there are older children who still need your love and attention. Let them in on all the fun with their baby brother or sister, but plan also to devote some time exclusively to them. Make it a point to buy little gifts for the older children whenever you buy a toy for the baby. Remember to ask them about their school and other activities. Take them on a special trip or outing occasionally, without the baby tagging along. A little extra attention to them at this time will go a long way in preventing deep resentment that may last throughout life.

Don't Forget Your Wife

Perhaps most important, remember that you have a wife, and that she is now also a mother. Don't let her do too much too soon. During her first two weeks at home, with her doctor's permission she can usually be up and around to care for herself and the baby. She should not be cooking elaborate meals, entertaining numerous guests, doing heavy housework, or performing such strenuous chores as the laundry. Don't encourage her to go on long shopping expeditions. If there are no relatives to help, or if she prefers not to call on them for assistance, you will be investing your money well if you hire someone to relieve her, at least during those hours of the day when you cannot be at home. If your wife does not give her muscles a chance to regain their tone before she uses them, she will feel draggy and droopy for months, and you will find that living with her is not too pleasant.

The Blues

Do not be surprised if your wife has occasional spells of the blues. All the excitement of pregnancy and birth is over. She is no longer getting the personal attention she received in the hospital. While you are at work, the days can seem awfully long and lonesome to her, especially while she is still physically under par. The care of the baby adds many duties which must somehow be squeezed into an already busy daily schedule. Many of these chores require skills that take time to acquire and an unaccustomed expenditure of energy. Is it any wonder that she will feel overwhelmed at times?

Don't add to her troubles. Learn to make the necessary adjustments to the situation. The night feedings will disturb your sleep, and the crying may get on your nerves. Your meals may not always be ready on time; they may not be as elaborate or as well prepared as they used to be. The house may not be as tidy or as quiet as it was when there were only two of you. Finally—and this is the hardest fact for many husbands to accept—you are no longer the sole object of your wife's love and attention. To add to all of these difficulties, you are not even permitted to have sexual relations for six whole weeks with the woman whom you love and who is once again so slim, beautiful, and desirable.

You will occasionally have moments when you'll feel that you made a mistake starting the entire thing. You will not be at all unusual—many new fathers have such feelings. The little bit of humanity that is the cause of all your troubles offers few satisfactions to compensate for the many ways in which he has disrupted your existence. The baby does not recognize you, does not smile at you, sometimes seems to scream in fear when you approach, does not do a thing to justify his presence except eat, cry, and sleep—mostly sleep.

But don't worry. Everything will be better than it ever was before. The family will settle into its new routine. With the aid of frozen foods, pre-packaged meals, occasional treats at a restaurant, and the new cooking skills that you will develop, you will eat as regularly and as well as you did before. With a little planning and scheduling so that you and your wife share the chores sensibly and equitably, you will start catching up on your sleep and will even find time to do some reading or to pursue some of your other hobbies. A little later, if you can't enlist the services of a mother or a mother-in-law as a babysitter, you may be able to hire a reliable one or make some exchange arrangement with a neighboring couple who have the same problem. As things calm down, your wife will become more skillful, confident, and relaxed in caring for the new baby. Soon she will even have some time for you, and before you know it she will hint that the doctor has told her that she is again physically capable of starting the whole thing over again. (By the way, if you swallow the old superstition that a woman cannot become pregnant while she is nursing a baby, you may discover that indeed you have started the whole thing over again before you expected or wanted to.)

The baby will begin to be part of your life, and pretty soon you will forget what it was like not to be a father. Of course, you will have to be patient and let the baby do a lot of growing before you can play ball with him or teach her how to dance or vice versa. But when your child starts to recognize you, to smile and make foolish noises when you enter the room, life will be richer than you ever imagined it could be. When you can take your wife out and resume your social, church and community life with the added spice of showing off the child in the carriage or at least displaying snapshots you will realize that marriage plus a baby is a good thing no matter how you look at it. Just keep calm during those first few weeks—parents always live through them.

CHAPTER 20

Family Planning

Most parents prefer to have their children one or two or more years apart. Some may want only one child, others may think they are cheaper by the dozen. At present there are a number of contraceptive methods so that you both can decide the means that suit you and your wife best.

The methods of contraception available for the male are:

1. *Coitus Interruptus.* This is withdrawal by the male during intercourse. Although popular in Europe some years ago, it is practiced in fewer than 5 percent of the population in the United States as the sole method of contraception. For some couples, however, withdrawal is the preferred method. The pregnancy rate is said to be eight to seventeen per hundred women per year of exposure. This rate compares favorably with fourteen for the condom and diaphragm and thirty-eight for the safe period.

While not recommending it as a good method of contraception, fewer physicians condemn coitus interruptus as a physically and psychologically injurious technique than in the past. For couples who both desire this method and have used it and are happy with it, there is no reason to discourage it, although the vulnerability of the method as far as pregnancy is concerned must be fully understood.

2. *Condom.* The condom is one of the oldest and most widely used contraceptives. Most men know about it, it is easily obtained, and it offers advantages not found in other techniques. It is the only method that also offers protection against venereal disease and fungal infections of the vagina. It also demonstrates its effec-

tiveness after each usage in that the sperm can be seen in the condom after each intercourse.

There are other advantages to the condom—instances where it is the method of choice. In cases of vaginal infections where there is likelihood of reinfection of the male, in cases in which anatomic conditions preclude the fitting of a diaphragm, in cases where the pill or the coil cannot be used, the condom may be the only available mechanical method of contraception. The condom may also be effective in cases of premature ejaculation in prolonging intercourse, and couples who have intercourse infrequently may find it convenient. It is without contraindications or side effects and has been estimated to be about 96 percent effective.

There are some men who refuse to use a condom because they say it decreases penile sensation or they must stop and put the condom on when they attain an erection and this interferes with their love-making. Failures from the use of the condom result from not using it at all or postponing its placement until later in coitus at the time of preejaculation at which time secretions of sperm may already have been produced or orgasm may already have occurred. Another danger is permitting the penis to remain in the vagina until it becomes completely soft when the chance of leakage from the now loose-fitting condom may take place.

3. *Surgical sterilization.* This consists of tying the vas or duct leading from the testicles to the urethra and penis. It is a simple procedure that can be done under local anesthesia. It has no side effects and is 100 percent effective. Only one precaution must be considered. Although intercourse can be resumed one week after the procedure, the male is not sterile immediately after vasectomy since mature sperm may remain in the vas deferens and accessory glands beyond the area of ligation. The man should have a semen examination eight weeks after the operation to make certain no sperm remain and the couple should use an adequate form of contraception during this time.

The operation should not be undertaken as a reversible procedure. The success rate in reversing it varies but is extremely small. The major side effect from vas ligation is psychological. The incidence of regret and dissatisfaction varies from 0 to 40 percent among published followups. One series reports 70 percent claimed to be happier and 2 percent were less happy. For many sex life improved while in others it was difficult to avoid equating vasectomy with castration.

Before undergoing the operation the man should be carefully evaluated, perhaps even by a psychiatrist, particularly if he has had any previous emotional disturbances. About 50 percent of those men who had a vasectomy were willing to have those around them know they had been sterilized, and less than a third recommended the operation to other men.

The consensus is that there is no evidence that couples after vasectomy were psychologically worse off than those couples who used other methods. Some men desired intercourse more frequently because they were concerned about their loss of masculinity and were attempting to compensate for it by increase in frequency of intercourse and other behavioral changes.

Undoubtedly the next few years will see major advances in contraceptive methods. The development of an oral contraceptive that can be taken by the male will be a tremendous breakthrough. The "morning after" pills are already in use for those "emergencies" when something has gone wrong with the usual contraceptive technique or none has been used. Other methods which are concerned with immunologic reaction are also being studied.

Family planning and management of the type of contraception is a continuing issue for most couples. Not infrequently, while both husband and wife may wish to avoid more children, the husband may desire more frequent intercourse than the wife and the wife may use fear of pregnancy in the absence of effective contraceptive methods as an excuse to avoid sexual relations. The thorough knowledge of contraception by the couple—both husband and wife—can avoid complex family problems. The issue as to who should be responsible for contraception must be determined by each couple. No longer should the man say to his wife, "That's your problem, I won't use a condom," a statement we have frequently heard from women coming in for their postpartum checkup.

A brief description of the mechanical methods of contraception for your wife is included so that you will be in a better position to select jointly the method that appeals to both of you.

1. Vaginal creams or foams. Vaginal creams or foams act as a mechanical barrier to the passage of the sperm to the cervix and

also act to kill those sperm that come in contact with it. Estimates of the efficiency of this method vary from 70 to 85 percent.

2. *Diaphragm*. This is a mechanical barrier used by the woman, usually together with a contraceptive cream—the latter being of importance in the effectiveness of this method since Masters and Johnson have shown that during sexual excitation even the best-fitting diaphragm moves quite freely in the vagina. The diaphragm can be inserted two to three hours before intercourse but must be left in place for at least eight hours after coitus. If intercourse occurs a second time within the eight-hour period, an additional application of contraceptive cream should be placed in the vagina without disturbing the diaphragm, which must be left in place for an additional eight hours. The diaphragm is considered to be 90 to 95 percent effective. Effectiveness varies with the length of time the method is used, for with increased experience there are fewer failures. Patient failures result when it is not used during every intercourse—particularly when intercourse catches a woman unprepared or when she skips a time relying on rhythm or the safe period. Method failure can occur when the female assumes the position on top of the male. The penis may be inserted between the diaphragm and the vaginal wall. In this position penile placement during either initial or subsequent mounting episodes should be checked by the female.

The diaphragm causes no systemic reaction and is safe with the exception of local irritation or allergy to the contraceptive cream. For those couples who try pills and wish to stop for several months, the diaphragm is very useful.

3. *IUD or intrauterine device*. As a result of refinement in both the type of device and technique of insertion the intrauterine device is being used by an increasing number of couples, particularly those who have just had a baby and wish to plan future pregnancies. It is much simpler to insert at the first postpartum visit or during the first menstrual period after the birth of the baby. For nursing mothers whose first menstrual period may be delayed it can be inserted any time after delivery at the discretion of the doctor.

At present the IUD is about 98 percent effective. The side effects such as increased menstrual flow and painful menses or intermenstrual spotting are infrequent and minor. They usually disappear in several months. If there is a preexisting pelvic infection this may flare up as a result of the insertion of an IUD and should be treated. The undesirable effects of the IUD, if any, are completely reversible when it is removed.

The IUD is particularly useful soon after pregnancy. It is the policy of many obstetricians to leave the IUD in for five years, if so requested, and replace it with a new one after one or two normal cycles.

4. *The pill.* The most effective method of contraception currently available is the oral contraceptive pill which contains the hormones estrogen and progesterone. In the customary dosage the pill is 100 percent effective. Tablets misused during cycles have accounted for about 1 pregnancy per 100 women per year.

The minor systemic effects such as nausea, breakthrough bleeding, scanty or absent menstrual flow, weight gain, and breast tenderness can usually be controlled by modification or change in the dosage. The presence of serious side effects such as elevation of blood pressure or blood sugar, occurrence of phlebitis or blood clots warrants immediate cessation of contraceptive pills. These complications can be avoided or treated and reversed by being under a doctor's supervision at regular intervals of not more than six months while the pill is used. In making an evaluation as to which patient should be given the pill the doctor considers the ability and willingness of the patient to communicate with him concerning any untoward effects.

There is no conclusive evidence that the pill is in any way a cause of cancer. As a matter of fact lives may be saved by bringing women into the doctor's office every six months for pelvic and breast examination and Pap smears.

5. *Rhythm.* One other method of joint responsibility of contraception should be mentioned; namely the rhythm method which is the only method presently approved by the Roman Catholic Church. For those who wish to practice the method a thorough discussion with their doctor is advisable.

CHAPTER 21

Toys for the Baby, Not for You

Fathers are sometimes teased about buying footballs and electric trains for their newborn sons, yet often their actual choice of toys for the young child is even more inappropriate. The head of a toy department in one of the world's largest stores points out that the most difficult job her salespeople face is not selling toys to fathers but discouraging them from buying the most unsuitable toys. One father, enchanted by a large doll with real blond hair and a complete wardrobe, insisted that this was just the thing to give to his infant daughter. It took quite an argument to persuade him that the little girl would be unable to handle a doll bigger than she was, that the elaborate costumes would be reduced to rags within a few days, and that the genuine hair would be a hazard to a young child. Another father stormed out of the same toy department when the salesgirl advised him that a mechanical construction set, complete with electric motor, was not at all suitable for a two-week-old boy. He insisted that his son was not a sissy who would be willing to play with the soft stuffed animal the salesperson suggested, and he left in search of a store where they understood boy babies and treated their fathers with proper respect!

The First Toys

For the first six weeks or so after the baby comes home, you will probably be the chief toy buyer in the family because your wife will be staying home caring for the baby. If you are like most men, you will continue to buy many of your child's toys throughout the years. Of course, relatives and friends will shower gifts upon the infant, and you can only hope that they will use their discretion or that they will heed the advice of experts. If you are foresighted, you will provide a safe storage place for objects that may be useful years hence, tactfully displaying them only when the donor visits. It might be a good idea, therefore, for you to learn a little about toys and their selection.

Toys have been in use since the first baby was born. In primitive societies mothers still give their infants a smooth stone to hold and suck or a dried and seed-filled gourd as a rattle. Without books or courses in child psychology, these mothers understand that children need toys. They know that babies like to touch smooth objects, place them in their mouths, and shake something that will make a gentle noise. Perhaps the latter is one means babies have of calling attention to the fact that they are very much present and alive. Dr. Grace Langdon, Child Development Adviser to the American Toy Institute, explains children's need for toys. "They need them to satisfy the ever-present urge to be active, to be up and doing. They need them for all of the investigating, exploring, experimenting, discovering, manipulating, creating, that is so much a part of growing."

At any given time in a child's life, there will be a variety of play interests that will last through the years and even into adulthood. These include active physical games, creative construction, dramatic imitation, play that employs skills and information, and both social and solitary activities. Examine your own recreational interests: you swim or play golf; you use your imagination, at least in doodling or in improvising simple household repairs; you get a kick out of imitating the boss to an audience; you solve crossword puzzles, listen to quiz programs or build things out of kits; you often go out with a group, but occasionally you prefer to read or listen to music in solitude. To carry on this large variety of pursuits, you need equally varied equipment. Similarly, your child, even during the first months of life, needs many different kinds of toys. However, these must be suited to his strength, coordination, attention span, changing interests, and especially to his individual personality. Toys must fit the child, and you must watch the child, play with him, and get to know him in order to select the toys he needs.

Within the first few weeks after the baby comes home, he will begin to grasp and reach for things and to notice sounds. This is the time for rattles of different sizes, shapes, and tones and for squeaky rubber animals and dolls. But don't feel that you have to buy all of these. You can save a good deal of money and get more pleasure out of improvising with common objects or building some of the toys yourself. An old tennis ball with a small puncture makes an excellent squealer and whoosher. Make the hole a little larger, insert a few beans or grains of rice, and plug the opening securely with plastic tape or some other material that won't fall out, and your baby has a first-rate rattle. But whenever you build or improvise, now or later, be conscious of safety. For example, a tobacco can does not make a safe rattle because its edges are likely to be razor sharp and the paint on it may be harmful. Babies have no judgment and everything they hold will eventually find its way into mouth, nose, eyes, or ears. You must be sure that their toys are either too large to be inserted into their body openings or that they will be harmless and easily removed if they do find their way in.

Very early in life, an infant has the urge to feel and squeeze, and later to hug and cuddle. A recent university study showed that baby monkeys deprived of their mothers were quite happy when they could nestle against a soft blanket, but rapidly pined away when they did not have such a substitute. Your wife cannot spend every waking moment with the baby, and soft woolly things in the crib will keep the infant happy. You must be careful that anything placed in the crib is fastened or arranged so that the child cannot wrap itself in it and suffocate. And remember, plastic bags used as containers for so many objects are a menace to babies because they cling to nose and mouth and have thus caused some deaths.

One of the best ways to provide safe fun is to fasten a few toys to the sides of the crib or suspend them across the rails. Babies love to stare at objects, especially brightly colored ones, and soon learn to reach for them, bat them around, and perform many other tricks. There are many such crib toys on the market, but here, too, you can improvise. Stretch a strong cord across the crib and hang on it objects such as curtain rings, small cardboard boxes and any other suitable items that you can find around the house. (Be sure the cords are not so long the baby can become tangled in them.) If you want to give your child a real treat and provide hours of amusement for yourself and your wife, tie a balloon to a crib bar. Be certain, however, that it is not too tightly inflated, for the bang that is sure to come after a while should not be too loud.

Bath toys are also important, especially with the rare infant who does not like water. Anything that floats is good. Plastic or rubber fish are very colorful, but a smooth chunk of light wood, the lid from a screw-top jar, or even a bar of floating soap is just as effective in keeping the baby happy. Your infant may enjoy playing with a soft rubber ear syringe and may learn how to squirt a stream of water with what seems to be uncanny accuracy.

And a Little Later

Very soon your baby will be able to sit up and hold things with a sure, firm grasp, turn objects this way and that, pass them from one hand to the other and even from his hands to yours. This is the time for small blocks of rubber, plastic, or wood. Experts suggest that it is a good idea to get colorful blocks, some with pictures on them, because very soon part of the child's fun will come from sorting the colors or looking at the pictures. Some children show amazing speed in identifying blocks and other toys by their colors or pictures. One baby loved to play with her picture books after her parents had read them to her at bedtime. Soon she developed the habit of sleeping with the books in her crib. One evening her mother accidentally left one of the books out of the crib, and the baby screamed with rage. When the book was replaced, the little girl calmed down. The father did not believe this story and decided to experiment. One night he removed a book from the crib while the child was asleep. When the baby awoke, the parents could hear her gurgling and cooing in her usual way, but soon there was a sudden silence followed by a wail. The father replaced the missing book and the child became happy again.

Books and records should be introduced almost at once. Of course your baby doesn't know what it is you are reading, but young infants like to hear your voice and the rustle of the pages.

Later they are intrigued by the brightly colored pictures, and enjoy the comfort and security of being held in your lap. Don't be surprised when one day baby tries to turn a page at the very moment it should be turned or whimpers a complaint if you decide to skip part of the story. No baby is too young for music. There are hundreds of suitable records, but many infants seem to prefer the music parents play for their own enjoyment. It really makes no difference—music is music, and seems to soothe the infant as well as the savage beast.

At the sitting and holding stage of development, your baby will learn to enjoy doing more complicated things with toys. If you provide a small basket or box, the baby will drop blocks or other toys into it one by one, tip them out, put them in again, and repeat the process endlessly, always seeking your approval and applause, which should be given lavishly. If there are nested boxes, beakers or measuring cups, the baby will take them apart and play with them separately at first. Then one day they will be piled one on top of the other, and finally there will be hit and miss efforts to get one inside the other. Before long they will be fitted together in their proper order.

By the end of the first year, or shortly after, your baby will be creeping or walking. This is the time for push-pull toys, animals on wheels, roller toys, a little light doll carriage, a small wagon. The musical, chiming push-pulls are good fun at this age. Simple take-apart-and-put-together toys satisfy the urge that baby—now really a youngster—has at this time to handle, investigate, and manipulate. Some children will be ready for the flat wooden trains without wheels that link together easily and can be pushed along as the child creeps. Peg cars with big, loosely fitted pegs provide hours of amusement to baby and parents alike, as do toys with blocks of varied shapes and sizes which can be slipped or pounded through the spaces provided for them.

Don't overlook the kitchen as a source of toys at this age. Just let your baby have freedom of the pot-and-pan closet and watch the fun. Small pots make receptacles for all sorts of things, and are ideal beach or sandbox toys for the young child. A healthy, vigorous infant with two lids can make a parent reach for earplugs. The brush type of push broom is an especially good toy. Not only will the baby believe that he is helping mother clean the house, but, in the process, will learn to use the broom as a support during early attempts at walking.

The most important toys, not only during the first years but for a long time thereafter, are a good father and mother. Talk to your baby. Sing to him. Rock your son or daughter in your arms. Lift the baby high in the air and swing him gently. Dance with your child. Play with him. Use the age-old games and invent new ones. Do anything with your baby that seems natural to you and that the child seems to enjoy. There is no substitute for your attention and your love.

CHAPTER 22

Babies Are Expensive

Most expectant fathers know that babies cost money, but few have any idea how much. Few realize that immediate cost is negligible compared to maintenance, and fewer still plan carefully and intelligently to meet their added financial responsibilities. The estimate of how much a girl costs, from her start at the hospital to her marriage, ranges from a few thousand dollars to fifty thousand dollars and more, depending on how indulgent the father can afford to be. There is no reason to suppose that boys are less expensive. This is not to imply that a baby isn't worth every dollar you will ever spend or that you should go into a panic as soon as you learn that your wife is pregnant. It is a good idea, however, to face the situation realistically, to discuss it with your wife, and to take whatever steps you can to solve the problem.

Certainly, you don't want to be guilty of the extremes described by one expert in family financial counseling. His client, a man who had struggled to achieve some degree of financial comfort and security, became almost a miser when he learned he was an expectant father. He insisted that family costs be cut to a minimum, even if this meant depriving his wife and himself not only of luxuries but of some bare necessities. He converted all of his investments into cash, some at a great loss. He went to the extent of canceling all his insurance policies, including those on his life, to provide immediate money for the coming baby. The counselor could not convince this man that he was doing the wrong thing financially and sought the cooperation of the obstetrician, who was finally able to persuade this husband that tensions created by such behavior might jeopardize the welfare of both mother and child. Another client felt that the nine months of his wife's pregnancy represented the last carefree period of his life and decided to go on a sustained spending binge. He stinted on nothing for his wife and especially for himself until he had so depleted his resources that a serious crisis threatened, not only in his economic situation but in his marriage. Fortunately, the financial counselor, having long known of this man's spendthrift habits, had been able to tie up some of the family funds so that they could not be touched without consent of both members. This saved the situation until the husband came to his senses.

Babies and Taxes

Before you go into a blue funk about the red-ink aspects of being a father, it may be heartening to consider the money that you will save on your income tax, for this is the only money you will ever save on a child. According to the law, a baby born at or before 11:59 P.M. December 31, 1972 entitles you to a $700. deduction for that year. In 1973 the deduction will be $750. Some obstetricians tell amusing stories of shrewd and calculating husbands who plan their families to take advantage of this provision of the income tax regulations. One husband whose wife was due to deliver early in January tried to convince the doctor to induce labor so that the baby would be born in time. Needless to say, the physician could not be convinced.

Since obstetrical care is included by the Internal Revenue Service in the list of "moneys paid out for the diagnosis, cure, treatment or prevention of disease," it can be listed along with your other medical expenses. Specifically deductible are:

a) visit to family doctor to confirm pregnancy

b) fees to him or to an obstetrician for prenatal care, delivery, and postnatal care

c) blood tests and urine analyses

d) vitamins and medicines if they exceed 1 percent of gross or adjusted income

e) all hospital expenses for mother and baby over and above those covered by insurance

f) cost of a nurse, including her salary, room and board, to care for mother and baby, but excluding that portion of the stipend paid for housework, cooking, and so on

g) ointments, creams, and other medications prescribed by the doctor for the treatment of such conditions as diaper rash, eczema, and prickly heat

h) diaper service if it is prescribed for a limited amount of time for a specific medical reason

i) cost of special corrective shoes, orthopedic appliances, and such, if they are prescribed by the doctor

j) cost of all transportation connected with treatment.

Don't go overboard in making deductions, for some are specifically prohibited. These include:

a) formula preparations, even if prescribed by the doctor

b) baby powders, lotions, and so on for ordinary daily use

c) fees paid to babysitters for older children while the mother is in the hospital

d) cost of a housekeeper, even if the use of one is recommended by a physician

e) cost of a "substitute mother" if your wife must take a job, except under certain circumstances that are so complicated they can best be explained by a tax expert who knows the facts in the individual case

f) cost of the baby's clothing.

When the April 15 deadline approaches, you will want to consider whether it is best to use the short form or whether you can save money by choosing the long form. You must remember, also, that you can only deduct medical and dental expenses that exceed 3 percent of your adjusted gross income. Also keep in mind that you can deduct the cost of medicines and drugs but only the amount that exceeds 1 percent of your adjusted gross income. Some fathers find that even if the long form saves money, this saving isn't enough to justify the brainracking and record-keeping involved, especially with the distraction of a new baby in the house. Finally, you will have to decide whether to file a joint return or individual returns for yourself and your wife. Usually the joint form operates to the advantage of the tax-paying couple and also avoids the bother of filling out two complicated statements instead of one. You will have to do a little preliminary arithmetic to decide what is best in your case.

Estimating Costs*

Now that you know about all the money your new baby is going to save you—it may amount to a few hundred dollars the first year and about half of that annually thereafter—take a deep breath! Now, try to estimate what your child will cost you immediately and over the years. More important, after you have caught your breath, try to make some plans after careful discussion with your wife. Since every family's financial circumstances are special, it is impossible to provide standard plans, budgets, and guidance. Nevertheless, certain basic information from authoritative sources and experienced financial counselors will help you to prepare a program suited to your own needs.

Consider your income from salary and all other sources. Chances are, you will have to depend solely on your own earnings for some time after the baby is born. If your wife has been employed, she will probably not return to her job right away and if there are more children later, not for many, many years. Even if she does go back to work, the need for additional household help created by her absence from the home may almost outweigh her earnings. Since the family income has been reduced, or at least has not been increased, there is a greater need now than ever before for proper financial management. Everything the family needs must be paid for. Whether the income is adequate depends not so much on actual take-home pay as on the balance sheet of wants on the one hand and resources on the other. The additional costs for the child may make it necessary to adjust yourselves to a new standard of living. This must be done as a result of frank discussion between you and your wife. If one of you makes the crucial decisions without consulting the other, there is bound to be dissatisfaction and discord. In any discussion on financial readjustment, remember that the baby is worth any sacrifice that you may be forced to make. These sacrifices are likely to be only temporary, but the rewards of successful parenthood are long-enduring.

* The general financial principles stated in this chapter are not likely to change materially over the years. Specific items, such as rent, food, hospital costs, and so on, may, however, be affected by economic fluctuations, tax law revisions, and other factors.

This is the time to budget needs against income. The most certain road to financial disaster, with its attendant personal and family unhappiness, is to live above your means. Of course you may be envious and even resentful of your neighbor or relative who has so many more material things than you can afford. Don't be tempted to compete! As your income increases from either job advancement or investment, you also will be able to own things and do things that you and your wife desire. But go slowly. Financial experts advise that you should always keep the rate of increased spending somewhat slower than the rate of increased earnings to provide for unexpected setbacks and to maintain a reserve of cash savings and solid resources such as life insurance. It is far more pleasant to raise your family's standard of living gradually than to be forced to lower it suddenly.

A budget cannot be based on a fixed concept. It must be sufficiently flexible to allow for changes in income and in expenditures. It will vary with your family's wants and needs, your education, the type of work you do and the standard of living your job requires, the community in which you live, your hobbies and interests, the organizations to which you belong, and now your hopes and aspirations for your child. The important thing to remember is that, with a limited income, spending must be based on some kind of budget, no matter how informal it may be. An experienced family financial counselor urges that you consider the following steps when you plan your budget.

1. Determine how much your income is. Include salary, dividends, interest, commissions, bonuses, and earnings from side jobs. Deduct income taxes, Social Security and other items that are taken directly out of your salary check.

2. Determine your unavoidable expenses. In addition to housing, heat, light, taxes other than income tax, insurance, installment debts, and transportation to and from work, include an amount set aside for major medical expenses.

3. Provide for savings. The equivalent of four weeks' income should be reserved for unforeseen emergencies. The purchase of a new home, repairs or home furnishings, college education for your children, vacations or retirement are large expenditures which require careful planning. You will be motivated to save if you write down the specific purpose for saving.

4. Estimate your day-to-day expenses. You should not forget such items as food, clothing, automobile, routine medical care, personal services such as laundry, cleaning, and the barber, minor household appliances and repairs, and personal allowances for all members of the family. Above all, don't overlook such things as church and organizational contributions, gifts, charity, and home entertaining.

In rewriting this chapter on costs I was impressed with how much medical and non-medical expenses for maternity care have risen in the past eight years. I discussed this with bank officials and insurance underwriters and some have suggested that they add maternity loans and family life insurance to their services. So if you suddenly become overwhelmed by the amount of money a new baby will cost, remember you can secure a loan to tide you over for several years. Most people buy their automobiles by taking loans, and cars cost more than having a baby—and don't last as long.

A Practical Budget Plan

To demonstrate how a budget might work out, one is presented below for a family of four with an annual income of $10,000 to $12,000. The figures are derived from the Bureau of Labor Statistics, United States Department of Labor, for the northeastern United States.

There was a noticeable rise of 12.6 percent from the spring 1967 standard of $9,977. (In August 1960, the budget for a similar family was $6,665, or 58 percent of the budget for 1969.) The major cause for this rise in living costs between 1967 and 1969 was the increase in taxes accounting for 32 percent of the added cost for such a family.

The figures for medical care were estimated at $300 in 1960, $512 in 1967 and $600 in 1969 for the moderate budget. This obviously indicates an increase of 100 percent for medical care in this decade. In actual practice however, the expenditures for medical care are less at lower income levels because many of these families either defer needed treatment or receive it in free clinics.

	SPRING 1969	SPRING 1967
Total budget	$ 11,236	$ 9,977
Total family consumption	8,589	7,857
Food	2,541	2,330
Housing	2,796	2,637
Transportation	855	771
Clothing & personal care	1,158	1,024
Medical care	600	512
Other family consumption	639	583
Personal income tax	1,703	1,300
All other*	944	820

* Includes gifts and contributions, personal life insurance, occupational expenses, Social Security, and disability.

Moreover, employers contribute some or all of the cost of group health insurance for most employees. Therefore, to calculate total medical care costs, 20 to 25 percent should be deducted to reflect the cost of insurance paid by employers.

A budget based on a family of four was deliberately selected for this book because the reader may have an older child or an additional dependent. If your family is smaller or larger, you can make adjustments as you will have to do in any event to meet your individual circumstances. Remember, too, the figures in the above budget are not for the purpose of blind duplication in your family, but as a guide to planning with your wife. The figure of approximately $11,250 is based on a family of four living in the northeastern United States and will vary in different parts of the country.

Aside from this general budget, you should prepare one dealing with immediate costs incurred as a direct result of the new baby. These, too, will vary among individuals and from community to community, but some approximations can be helpful.

Medical and Hospital Fees

	RANGE	AVERAGE
Obstetrical care	$ 250–500	$ 350
Hospitalization for five days (Hospital insurance will cover part of this)	550–885	700
Special medications and vitamins	75–125	100
	$ 875–1510	$ 1150

Hospital Expenses

As soon as you can, find out what your hospital expenses are going to be. Know exactly what each item includes, how payment is to be made, and when payments are due. Some hospitals make separate charges for the delivery room, for anesthetics, and for nursing care of mother and baby. Other hospitals charge a lump sum that covers everything. Have a clear understanding about this so that you will not be surprised later by bills you did not expect.

You may have hospital insurance or belong to some group that provides hospitalization for its members. In this case reread your policy carefully, including the fine print, to be sure just what it covers. If you do not have such insurance, and sometimes even if you do, your hospital may require a cash deposit when your wife enters.

You must also consider such items as the layette, furniture, and accessories aside from toys. According to a list of prices obtained from Macy's department store buyer in March 1972, the cost of these items ranges as follows:

Baby Furnishings

Layette	$ 50–130
(a package costs about $80–85)	
High chair	20–45
Playpen	20–45
Bathinette	20–30
Dressing table	25–45
Crib	35–140
Bassinet	12–25
Stroller	20–50
Carriage	40–150
	$ 262–660

According to the National Center for Health Statistics, Division of Vital Statistics, the $1500 baby arrived in 1968. Typical fees to obstetrician and pediatrician for the baby's first week of life were less than what it cost to outfit the newcomer. The cost of outfitting mother and child was $681.44, which was higher than the hospital expenses of $576.87 for room, delivery room, nursery, and circumcision.

In 1970 a baby was born in the United States every seven and a half seconds. Each began life by screaming loudly in a voice that will be heard for some seventy years. "He is screaming for 26,000,000 tons of water, 21,000 gallons of gasoline, 10,150 pounds of meat, 28,000 pounds of milk and cream, 9,000 pounds of wheat, and great storehouses of all other foods, drinks and tobaccos. These are his life-time demands of his country and its economy."*

* From Robert and Leona Train Rienow, *Moment in the Sun* (New York: Dial Books, 1967).

College Is Costly

Even though you are probably reeling by this time, you had better do some thinking about the future, at least the next eighteen to thirty years, depending on whether you are planning to have more children and on what you hope to do for them. Disregarding such things as nursery school, camp, sweet-sixteen parties, and weddings, just consider the matter of college. Since averages are usually deceiving, it may be more helpful to look at the costs of various types of colleges in different parts of the country.

One of the "big three"	$4240
A prestigious small Eastern men's college	3525
A good Eastern women's college	3900
An Eastern engineering school	3220
A Southern state university	3360
A Midwestern state university (residents)	1650
(non-residents)	2950
A private Midwestern university	3525
A Pacific-coast private university	3385

The estimated costs for one year include only tuition, matriculation fees, room, board, books, and supplies. To these, you must add clothing, transportation, and spending money, the last of which comes very high according to parents of college students. These estimated costs are based on the figures for 1969. All authorities agree that college education will become more expensive over the next decade. As a matter of fact, a notice received from one of the colleges listed above advised a 1970 increase of $200 in tuition and $250 for board.

Now the question arises as to how to provide for future needs such as college education. It is most important for the young and growing family to keep up its cash savings as an emergency reserve and for working capital. Equally important is to maintain and increase your life insurance protection. Every life insurance company has many basic plans as well as several variations within each plan. It is important to secure the advice of a qualified insurance counselor who will establish a plan for you after determining your particular needs and ability to pay.

Family financial counselors are unanimous in urging everyone, especially young husbands just starting their families, not to venture into investments of any kind unless they have adequate savings and insurance. With that done, it is time to develop an intelligent investment portfolio to provide income and asset growth that savings and insurance cannot furnish. Any investment program activated by a "get rich quick" motive is likely to fail, so choose your investments wisely. Invest in sound stocks whose future growth will pace the country's growth. Remember, you should plan for the long haul. The best way to secure further information about investments in stocks, savings accounts, and funds, is to consult with a representative of a reliable bank or insurance company in your community.

Finally, most financial counselors will agree with doctors, psychologists, and social agencies that parents ought to think of themselves as well as of their children. Those who deprive themselves of minor luxuries and even necessities to provide unusual benefits for their children are making a serious mistake. Even if only subconsciously, the parents are bound to be resentful, and this is likely to interfere with the good relationship that is at the very basis of the happy family. You and your wife must enjoy having a baby and raising a child; anything that lessens or destroys that enjoyment is bad for all concerned. So plan for your child's future but don't neglect the present and your own future.

Names, Names, Names

With a Note on Selection

When Shakespeare asked, "What's in a name?" and implied in his answer that names were not really significant, he was making a serious mistake! You and your wife will select the baby's name, but the child will have to carry it through life or undergo legal proceedings to change it. A perfectly lovely girl was tortured in high school and college because although her parents didn't bother to look up the meaning of the name they gave her, her classmates did. The mother, whose interest in gardening took the form of reading about it rather than practicing it, thought it would be a charming idea to name her daughters after herbs. The first child was named Angelica and the second Rosemary, both very acceptable names for young ladies. The third, however, was called Henbane, which refers to a foul-smelling herb with sticky, hairy leaves and an unattractive flower that is a deadly poison. If you check the meaning of a name, especially one that is unusual, in an unabridged dictionary, you will avoid such a calamity.

Even the subterfuge of using only the initial of an undesirable name is likely to backfire. It sometimes inspires friends and acquaintances to arduous research that uncovers the secret, and then the bearer of the name is really in for it. One dignified executive who called himself A. Roger not only lost much of his dignity but was subjected to all sorts of good-natured but painful ribbing when a subordinate spread the news that the A stood for Adalbert.

You and your wife should select a name for the baby as early as possible, considering alternative names to take care of either sex. Sometimes, it may be advisable to think of the possibility of twins. The list provided here may help you with some ideas, but you certainly should be prepared for a quick decision. In some cities, authorities insist that the birth certificate, including name, be completed within hours after the baby is born. In other communities, there is more time for a decision, but the hospital is not the best place to arrive at one.

As a father, you will often be called on to help your child in moments of crisis or great need. The moment when the baby's name is chosen may be the first of these unless you and your wife join forces for the sake of a helpless infant who cannot protect its own interests. Both your families may conspire against the three of you, especially if the baby is a first grandchild on either side. Stand firm! Even though there may be a long family tradition, don't name a child of the twentieth century Increase or Zerubbabel. Even though a maiden aunt or a bachelor cousin may be enormously wealthy and in precarious health, don't name the baby Erasmus or Murdeena. Furthermore, don't let the baby become a victim of fads. You may think it is a fine tribute to a national hero to name your son after him, but when the boy grows up and half the boys in his class have the same name, he may not be too happy about it. Similarly, while names of the popular wives and daughters of presidents are usually fine, they will lose their appeal when the administration changes.

Don't try to be too distinctive or individual. Most children, when they grow up, are happiest with the good old names drawn primarily from the Bible, Western history, or various national, religious, and ethnic traditions. The Davids and the Johns, Ruths and Deborahs, Williams and Edwards, Marys and Janes are seldom embarrassed by their names. The Heliotropes, Artemisias, and Zelmiras frequently are. Nor should you let your hobbies or special interests tempt you to choose an uncomfortable name for your child. The children of an opera lover hated music for the rest of their lives, largely because they had been named Brünnhilde, Euridice, Leporello, and Papageno. Try to make sure that you don't choose a name that is easily converted into an embarrassing nickname. Think of what could be done with Fatima, Deauport, and Stinchfield if you were foolhardy enough to give these names to your child. On the other hand, some names are deliberately selected because they make good nicknames, and parents plan never to use full names. Nevertheless, other people may not be as kind, and Candy, Randy, and Sandy may be forced to go through life being called Candelia, Mirandella, and Sandisfield. If you want to use a nickname that appeals to you, by all means do it, but assign it to your child legally, and with full knowledge that it may cause some confusion. Furthermore, don't hesitate to use any unusual or meaningful name that you may invent or that has been used in your family for years. Just be sensible about it.

Finally, bear in mind that you also have a last name, and that your child will have to use the combination of first and last name. Listen to the first names you are considering linked to your last name. Some just do not go together. Then be sure that the initials don't spell RAT or something equally embarrassing.

With the preceding cautionary note, the following list of names is presented, not so much to make the choice of your child's name easy as to remind you of a few that you may have forgotten and to suggest new possibilities. Many of the boys' names can be feminized, sometimes with a little alteration in spelling: for example, Daniel to Danielle; Simon to Simone; Robert to Roberta. Most of the common names can be translated into non-English versions; for example, John to Jean, Juan, Jan, and Sean. The list was prepared after careful search of the student rosters of many schools and colleges. It was checked with one hundred teenagers in a typical high school, and any name that was found objectionable by more than two boys or girls was eliminated. The list is by no means exhaustive, and it is clearly labeled: USE WITH CARE!

Boys' Names

Aaron	Albert	Alvin	Antonio
Abner	Alexander	Ambrose	Armand
Abraham	Alexis	Amos	Arnold
Adam	Alfred	Andrew	Arthur
Adrian	Allister	Angelo	Asa
Alan	Alvah	Anthony	Asher

Aubrey	Clyde	Ezekiel	Hiram
Austin	Conrad	Ethan	Homer
Avery	Craig	Eugene	Howard
	Curtis	Everett	Howell
Baldwin	Cyril	Ezra	Hubert
Barry	Cyrus		Hugh
Baruch		Felix	Humphrey
Basil	Dale	Floyd	
Bayard	Daniel	Francis	Ira
Benedict	David	Frank	Irvin
Benjamin	Dean	Franklin	Irving
Bernard	Dennis	Frederick	Irwin
Bertram	Denton		Isaac
Bertrand	Derek	Gabriel	Isaiah
Blake	Dexter	Garrett	Israel
Blane	Dominic	Gary	Ivan
Boyd	Donald	Geoffrey	
Brian	Douglas	George	Jacob
Bronson	Dudley	Gerald	James
Bruce	Duncan	Gerard	Jason
Bryan	Dwight	Gilbert	Jasper
Burton		Giles	Jay
Byron	Earl	Glenn	Jeffrey
	Edgar	Godfrey	Jeremiah
Caleb	Edmund	Gordon	Jerome
Calvin	Edward	Graham	Jesse
Carl	Edwin	Grant	Joel
Carlton	Eli	Gregory	John
Cary	Elijah	Griffith	Jon
Cecil	Elliot	Grover	Jonathan
Cedric	Ellis	Guy	Jordan
Charles	Elton		Joseph
Chester	Emery	Hal	Judah
Christopher	Emil	Harlan	Julian
Clair	Emmanuel	Harold	Julius
Clarence	Enos	Harrison	
Clark	Ephraim	Harry	Karl
Claude	Eric	Harvey	Keith
Clayton	Ernest	Hector	Kelvin
Clement	Errol	Henry	Kenneth
Clifford	Erskine	Herbert	Kent
Clinton	Erwin	Herman	Kevin

Kirk	Maurice	Ralph	Taylor
Kurt	Maury	Randall	Terence
	Max	Raphael	Thaddeus
Lambert	Melvin	Raymond	Thane
Lance	Michael	Reginald	Theobold
Lawrence	Miles	Reuben	Theodore
Lester	Milton	Richard	Thomas
Lee	Mitchell	Robert	Thornton
Leif	Mordecai	Roderick	Timothy
Leland	Morgan	Rodney	Titus
Lemuel	Murray	Roger	Tobias
Leo	Myron	Ronald	Tracy
Leon		Ross	
Leonard	Nathan	Rowland	Urban
Leopold	Neal	Roy	
Leroy	Nelson	Rudolph	Vernon
Leslie	Nicholas	Rufus	Victor
Levi	Nigel	Rupert	Vincent
Lewis	Noah	Russell	Virgil
Lincoln	Noel		Vivian
Lionel	Norman		
Llewellyn	Norris	Samson	
Louis		Samuel	Wade
Lorenz		Sanford	Waldo
Lucius	Oliver	Saul	Wallace
Ludwig	Orrin	Scott	Walsh
Luke	Orville	Sebastian	Walter
Luther	Oscar	Selig	Warren
Lyle	Osmund	Seth	Wayne
Lynn	Oswald	Seymour	Wendell
	Otto	Sheldon	Wesley
Malcolm	Owen	Sidney	Wilbur
Manfred		Silas	Wilfred
Manuel	Patrick	Silvester	Willard
Marcus	Paul	Simeon	William
Marion	Perry	Simon	Willis
Mark	Peter	Solomon	Winston
Marshall	Philip	Stanley	Winthrop
Martin	Preston	Steven	Woodrow
Marvin		Stewart	
Matthew	Quentin	Sumner	Zachary

Girls' Names

Abby	Betty	Delphine	Fay
Abigail	Beulah	Denise	Felicia
Ada	Blanche	Diana	Fern
Adele	Bonnie	Diantha	Flora
Adeline	Brenda	Dolores	Florence
Adrienne	Bridget	Donna	Frances
Agatha		Dora	Freda
Agnes	Camille	Doris	Frederica
Alexandra	Carlotta	Dorothea	
Alfreda	Carmella	Dorothy	Gail
Alice	Carmen		Genevieve
Aline	Carol	Edith	Georgia
Alma	Caroline	Edna	Geraldine
Althea	Catherine	Eileen	Germaine
Amanda	Cecilia	Elaine	Gertrude
Amelia	Celeste	Eleanor	Gilda
Amy	Celia	Elizabeth	Ginger
Andrea	Charlotte	Ellen	Gladys
Angela	Cheryl	Elissa	Gloria
Angelica	Christine	Eloise	Grace
Ann	Claire	Elsa	Greta
Annabel	Clara	Elsie	Gretchen
Annette	Clarissa	Elva	Gretel
Antoinette	Claudia	Emeline	Guinevere
Arabella	Colleen	Emily	Gwendolyn
Arlene	Constance	Emma	Gwynneth
Astrid	Cora	Enid	
Audrey	Coral	Erma	Hannah
Augusta	Corinne	Ernestine	Harriet
Avis	Corliss	Estelle	Hazel
	Cornelia	Esther	Heather
Barbara	Cynthia	Ethel	Helen
Beatrice	Cyrena	Etta	Henrietta
Belinda		Eugenia	Hermione
Belle	Daisy	Eva	Hester
Bernice	Daphne	Evangeline	Hetty
Bertha	Deborah	Evelyn	Hilda
Beryl	Deirdre		Hildegarde
Beth	Delia	Faith	Hope

Hortense	Kim	Marjorie	Pamela
		Marlene	Patience
Ida	Laura	Martha	Patricia
Ilsa	Laurel	Mary	Paula
Imogene	Lauren	Matilda	Pauline
Inez	Leah	Maud	Pearl
Ione	Leila	Mavis	Penelope
Irene	Lenore	Maxine	Philippa
Iris	Leslie	Melanie	Phoebe
Irma	Letitia	Melba	Phyllis
Isabelle	Libby	Melinda	Portia
Iseult	Lillian	Melissa	Priscilla
Ivy	Linda	Mercedes	Prudence
	Lois	Merry	
Jacqueline	Lola	Michelle	Rachel
Jan	Loretta	Mildred	Ramona
Jane	Lorna	Millicent	Rebecca
Janet	Lorraine	Minerva	Regina
Janice	Louise	Miranda	Renée
Jean	Lucette	Miriam	Rhea
Jeanette	Lucia	Mitzi	Rhoda
Jennifer	Lucille	Moira	Roberta
Jessica	Lucinda	Molly	Robin
Jessie	Lucretia	Monica	Rochelle
Jill	Lucy	Muriel	Rosa
Joan	Luella	Myra	Rosalie
Joanne	Lydia	Myrna	Rosalind
Josephine	Lynne		Rose
Joy		Nancy	Rosemary
Joyce	Mabel	Nanette	Rowena
Joyceann	Madeline	Naomi	Roxanne
Juanita	Mae	Natalie	Ruby
Judith	Magdalene	Nina	Ruth
Julia	Marcella	Nola	
Juliana	Marcia	Nora	Sally
Juliet	Margaret	Norma	Sandra
June	Margot		Sarah
Justina	Marguerite		Selby
	Marian	Octavia	Selina
Karen	Marie	Olga	Selma
Katherine	Marietta	Olive	Sharon
Kathleen	Marilyn	Olivia	Sheila

Sherry	Sylvia	Ursula	Virginia
Shirley			Vivian
Shulamith	Terry	Valerie	Wanda
Sigrid	Tess	Velina	Wendy
Sophia	Thea	Velma	Willa
Stella	Theodora	Vera	Wilma
Stephanie	Thelma	Verna	Winifred
Susan	Tilda	Veronica	Yvonne
Suzanne	Tina	Vesta	
Suzette	Toby	Victoria	Zelda
Sybil		Vida	Zina
Sydelle	Una	Violet	Zoe

Doctors' Language

An Informal Guide to Obstetrical Terms

This brief and admittedly incomplete glossary of obstetrical terms is presented not only because most obstetricians use them in talking to pregnant women and their husbands, but because they are likely to be used in books and magazines, on radio and television, and especially in conversation with other experienced expectant fathers and mothers. The considerate physician is usually careful to make himself clear to his patient; the layman often takes delight in displaying medical knowledge he has acquired by flaunting the vocabulary of the profession. You can use this glossary to impress other expectant fathers with your erudition or as an aid in understanding what you read and hear. The latter is recommended.

(The use of italics indicates that a term is defined in its proper alphabetical place in this list.)

Abdomen: The body region between the lower rib margin and the pubic bone; the belly. (The latter term is perfectly polite and proper.)

Abortion: The medical term for early miscarriage. Termination of pregnancy prior to the period of viability.

Achondroplastic Dwarfism: A bone disorder characterized by shortness of stature, a large head, stubby hands, and a deformity of the spine.

Aftercare: Medical and nursing care of the mother after birth of the baby. Sometimes called postnatal or postpartum care.

Afterbirth: See *Placenta*.

Albumin: A body substance that is normally found in the blood but which occasionally appears in the urine if the kidneys are not functioning properly. (This is one of the substances for which the doctor looks when he examines your wife's urine specimen.)

Allele: The mate of a gene in the opposite chromosome of the pair.

Amniocentesis: The aspiration of fluid from the bag of waters surrounding the fetus by passing a needle through the abdominal wall of the mother.

Amniography: The visualization of the soft tissues of the fetus on X-ray following the injection of a radio-opaque substance into the amniotic cavity. It is useful to detect congenital anomalies not visible on ordinary X-ray film.

Amnioscopy: The visualization of amniotic fluid through the cervix. It is also a procedure for direct visualization of the fetus by inserting a narrow tube-like instrument through the mother's abdominal wall into the bag of waters. The latter procedure is useful for intrauterine transfusions in Rh-sensitized fetuses.

Amniotic Fluid: A clear or somewhat milky liquid in which the baby floats while it is in the uterus. The fluid helps to cushion the fetus against outside shocks, allows unhampered growth and movement, and serves as an insulator against heat and cold. This fluid, which varies in amount from one to three pints at term, escapes when the membranes containing it either rupture spontaneously or are broken by the doctor during the course of labor or delivery.

Analgesic: A drug, gas, or other agent that relieves or reduces pain without causing unconsciousness.

Anemia: A condition of the blood in which there is either not enough hemoglobin or not enough red blood cells.

Anesthetic: A drug, gas, or other agent which is used to prevent pain. There are two kinds: general and local. General anesthetics are used to induce sleep; local anesthetics are injected beneath the skin into muscle or other tissues, or into the spinal canal, to desensitize special areas of the body.

Antepartum: The period of pregnancy from conception to delivery. Frequently used as an adjective in such expressions as antepartum care.

Anus: The opening of the rectum.

Autosome: A chromosome other than an X or a Y.

Bag of Waters: The common term for the sac of membranes attached to the placenta and filled with fluid that encloses the baby in the uterus.

Barr Bodies: Small, dark staining masses (chromatin masses) visible on the X chromosome. The presence of these masses indicates a female child.

Birth Canal: The passageway through which the baby emerges from the uterus, comprising the cervix, the vagina, and the vulva.

Bladder: The organ that collects and stores urine as it drains down from the kidneys, and from which the urine passes out of the body.

Braxton Hicks Contractions: The painless uterine contractions that occur every half hour or so from the fifth month of pregnancy to the onset of labor.

Breech Delivery: A delivery in which the baby is born feet or buttocks first. (Modern obstetrical techniques make this type of delivery so safe that mothers no longer fear or boast about it.)

Caesarean Section: The surgical procedure whereby the baby is delivered through an incision in the abdomen rather than through the birth canal. (Contrary to popular belief, the operation was not performed for the first time at the birth of Julius Caesar. It is far older but so called because of the eminence of the Roman ruler who was allegedly born in this manner.)

Catheterization: A technique whereby a small, flexible tube is passed through the urethra and into the bladder to draw out urine. (If you have undergone this procedure, you will be happy to know that, in contrast to the experience for men, it is almost painless for women.)

Cervix: The lower end of the uterus containing the os, or opening into the vagina. Sometimes called the neck of the uterus.

Circumcision: Surgical removal of the foreskin of the penis. (Once practiced primarily among Jews and Mohammedans, this procedure has gained almost universal acceptance for excellent medical and hygienic reasons.)

Colostrum: The thin, watery fluid which begins to seep from the nipples about the fourth month of pregnancy, and which serves to nourish the baby after birth until milk begins to form.

Conception: The union of the male and female sex cells.

Conceptus: The whole product of conception at any stage of development, from fertilization of the egg to birth.

Contraction: The tightening of the uterine muscles that plays a major role in delivery of the baby. Uterine contractions earlier in pregnancy, which can be felt but are painless, are called Braxton Hicks contractions and do not indicate onset of labor.

Coccyx: The very last portion of the spinal column, sometimes referred to as the "tail bone."

Dilatation: The stretching of the cervix in labor.

Dominant Gene: One of a pair of alternative genes capable of masking the effect of the other when both are present in the same cell. It can produce a recognizable birth defect. Dominant disorders are passed from generation to generation. An example is achondroplastic dwarfism.

Down's Syndrome: See *Mongolism*.

Episiotomy: A small cut at the vaginal entrance made by the doctor at the birth of the baby so that the mother's tissues will not be torn or otherwise injured. The incision is repaired immediately and is generally healed by the time the mother is ready to leave the hospital.

Estriol: One of the female sex hormones excreted in small amounts during the menstrual cycle but in large amounts during pregnancy. Since it increases in the urine and blood of the pregnant woman, it is useful in determining placental function and monitoring the fetus during pregnancy.

Fallopian Tubes: The two small tubes leading from the ovaries to the uterus. Conception usually takes place in these tubes as the egg meets the sperm. The fertilized egg then passes down into the uterus, where it spends the remainder of the gestation period.

Fertilization: See *Conception*.

Fetal Heart: Actually, the heart of the baby while in the uterus, but generally applied to the heartbeat which the doctor can hear when he places his stethoscope against the mother's abdomen.

Fetology: A new branch of medicine dealing with diagnosis in the unborn infant. It is concerned with the fetus and his environment, and its practitioners use hormonal, biophysical, cytologic, X-ray, and sonar techniques to make determinations.

Fetus: The term used for the baby in the uterus during the last six months of pregnancy.

Fontanel: A soft spot on the top of the baby's head where skull bones have not yet grown together. This makes it possible for the head to be compressed without injury during birth, and also permits growth of the head after birth. Closure of these spots takes place as early as nine months and as late as two years, the average being twelve to eighteen months.

Forceps: An obstetrical instrument which the doctor sometimes uses to help lift the baby's head out of the birth canal.

Fundus: The top of the uterus.

Gene: A hereditary germinal unit in the chromosome.

Genitals, Genitalia: Sex organs.

Gestation: The act or period of carrying the baby in the uterus; pregnancy.

Gonad: Ovary or testes.

Gravida: The medical term for a pregnant woman, usually used on hospital records. A woman pregnant for the first time is referred to as a primigravida. The gravidity of a woman is always considered independent of her parity.

Hemagglutination-Inhibition (H.I.) Test: A blood test to determine whether antibodies against German measles are present.

Hemoglobin: The red chemical in blood cells which is concerned with carrying oxygen. (See *Anemia*.)

Hemorrhoids: Piles or varicose veins of the rectum.

High-Risk Baby: A fetus or newborn whose mother is exposed to one or more of the complications of pregnancy, such as diabetes, toxemia, Rh disease, and who is in a precarious condition.

High-Risk Pregnancy: A general category which is characterized by complications including diabetes, toxemia, Rh disease, and previously poor obstetric history. It carries an increased risk of infant mortality and morbidity.

Huntington's Chorea: A degenerative disease of the brain appearing late in life. It is characterized by irregular fidgeting movements, especially when under stress.

Involution: The return of the uterus to normal size after birth of a baby. This process is usually complete in five or six weeks and is hastened if the mother nurses the baby.

Labor: The stage of birth which is marked by regular contractions of the uterus, opening of the cervix, and changes in the birth canal so that the baby can pass through.

Laceration: Tear, usually of the tissues near the vagina, as the baby is born. Episiotomy is performed to prevent this.

Lactation: The process of producing and supplying milk.

Lamaze Method: See *Psychoprophylaxis*.

Lanugo: The fine, hair-like down that appears on the body of the newborn baby. This eventually falls out.

Lightening: The sensation that the mother feels when the baby settles lower down in the pelvis toward the end of pregnancy.

Lochia: The discharge of blood and other materials from the uterus after birth of the baby. This may continue for several weeks.

LSD: Lysergic acid diethylamide. A powerful hallucinogenic drug which may have a harmful effect on the offspring when taken by the pregnant woman.

Lunar Month: A period of twenty-eight days which is always used in measuring any time sequence related to a woman's sexual functions. While pregnancy is ordinarily considered to take nine months, actually ten lunar months elapse between conception and delivery.

Maternity Care: The care of the mother during the prenatal period, at labor and delivery, and after the baby's birth.

Meconium: The newborn baby's normally black bowel movement.

Membranes: See *Bag of waters.*

Menstruation: The regular monthly flow of blood from the uterus and through the vagina which occurs in the non-pregnant woman during childbearing years.

Miscarriage: The loss of the embryo or fetus during early months of pregnancy, before it has reached a stage of development at which it could possibly live. (See *Abortion* and *Stillbirth.*)

Mongolism (*Down's Syndrome*): A type of mental retardation caused by chromosomal abnormalities. It is characterized by a peculiar conglomeration of physical traits which include "mongoloid" eye slant, abnormally shaped ears, fat pad on neck, characteristic patterns of palms and soles, and other physical defects.

Morning Sickness: The feeling of nausea or discomfort which sometimes comes during the first three months of pregnancy.

Mosaicism: Two or more cell populations with differing chromosome complements. This may result from chromosomal nondisjunction or other faults in an early division of the zygote.

Mucous Membrane: The thin, moist tissue that lines the vagina as well as other organs, such as mouth, nose, and digestive tract.

Mucus: The colorless, sticky material secreted by glands in certain parts of the mucous membrane to keep it moist.

Multigravida: A woman who has been pregnant several times.

Multipara: A woman who has had two or more children.

Mutation: The change that a gene undergoes with the result that it no longer functions in its usual manner.

Nausea: A feeling of discomfort, usually centered in the region of the stomach, which often leads to vomiting. (The word *nauseous*, often misused as a synonym for *nauseated*, really means the causing of a feeling of nausea. Thus, "I am nauseous!" means that the speaker is causing a feeling of nausea in his listeners.)

Nullipara: A woman who has never been pregnant.

Obstetrician: A doctor who specializes in the care of pregnant women and the delivery of babies.

Ovaries: The two small internal organs which produce the female egg cells.

Ovum: The female sex cell. (Plural, ova.)

Palpation: The technique whereby an examining physician feels with his hands for certain signs that help him determine what is going on in the body.

Para: Refers to past pregnancies that have reached the stage of viability. The parity of a woman refers not to the number of times she has been pregnant but to the number of times she has actually given birth to a living child by way of the birth canal. See *Multipara, Nullipara, Primipara.*

Pelvic Examination: Internal examination of the uterus and the ovaries.

Pelvic Measurements: The dimensions of the birth canal. These are estimated by the doctor and help him plan the delivery.

Pelvic Organs: The organs of the woman's body which are contained within the hollow of the pelvic bones. These include the uterus, vagina, ovaries, Fallopian tubes, bladder, and rectum.

Pelvis: The circle of bones forming the support of the upper body and to which the leg bones are attached.

Perineal Care: Cleansing of the perineum.

Perineum: The tissues surrounding the anus and the vagina.

Phenylketonuria (PKU): A condition in newborn infants caused by an excess of the amino acid phenylalanine. If unrecognized and untreated, it results in mental retardation.

Pitocin: One of the hormones of the pituitary gland. In obstetrics, this hormone may be used in three ways: to induce labor; to cause contraction of the uterus after birth of the baby and placenta; to hasten the production of milk.

Placenta: A cake-shaped organ which is attached to the lining of the uterus. The baby is attached to this through the umbilical cord and thus secures nourishment while it is in the uterus. The placenta weighs about one pound and is expelled shortly after birth of the baby.

Postpartum: An adjective designating the period after birth of the baby. Thus, postpartum care and examination.

Postpartum Examination: Examination of the pelvic organs, especially to determine whether they are returning to normal after birth of a baby.

Pregnancy: The period of time from conception to birth or abortion.

Premature: A baby weighing less than five and a half pounds.

Premature Labor: The onset of labor before the thirty-sixth week of pregnancy. This is one of the great problems in obstetrics. The earlier in gestation premature labor occurs the greater the infant mortality.

Presentation: The aspect of the baby's body that first appears at the external opening of the birth canal. Thus, breech and vertex presentations and deliveries.

Primigravida: A woman who is pregnant for the first time.

Primipara: A woman who has given birth to one child.

Psychoprophylaxis: A method of preparation for childbirth using both psychological and physical techniques. Its basic principles are education, understanding, preliminary exercises, and a technique of special breathing activity and relaxation during labor.

Pubic Bones: The front bones of the pelvis.

Puerperium: The period following delivery—about six weeks.

Recessive Gene: That one of a pair of alternative alleles whose effect is masked by the activity of the second when both are present in the same cell. Mutation must occur at both a gene and its mate (allele) in order to produce a recognizable effect. Examples include cystic fibrosis or phenylketonuria.

Rectum: The lower end of the bowel.

Rh Factor: A substance present in the red blood cells of most persons.

Rooming-in: A method of hospital care where the newborn infant spends most of its time at the bedside of the mother rather than in the nursery.

Sex Chromatin: In females XX there is a special mass of chromatin situated next to the nuclear membrane. It is derived from one of the two X chromosomes and is female-specific because it is lacking in the nuclei of males XY. As a rule about two-thirds of the cells of female origin are chromatin positive (Barr).

Show: The popular term for the small amount of mucus and blood which comes out of the vagina early in labor and is often the first sign of its onset.

Spermatozoon: The male sex cell. (Plural, spermatozoa.)

Sphincter: A circular muscle at the end of certain hollow organs, such as the anus, which can open and shut tight.

Sphygmomanometer: The instrument with which the doctor measures blood pressure.

Stethoscope: The instrument through which the doctor can hear heartbeats, breath sounds, and other internal noises.

Stillbirth: A fetus or baby born dead after reaching the period of viability.

Tay-Sachs Disease: A rare fetal disease of the nervous system that affects infants before the first year of age. It is characterized by progressive mental deterioration, blindness, motor paralysis, and spasticity.

Term: The usual end of pregnancy.

Trimester: A three-month period during pregnancy. Pregnancy is usually divided into three trimesters, each having certain characteristics and significance.

Toxemia: A complication of pregnancy associated with high blood pressure, swelling of the hands and feet, and albumin in the urine.

Translocation: Fusion of parts or all of two chromosomes resulting in a fetal anomaly.

Umbilical Cord: The cylindrical cord of blood vessels and other tissues which is attached at one end to the baby's abdomen and at the other to the placenta. The circulation of blood through this cord provides the oxygen and nutrients necessary for the baby while it is in the uterus.

Umbilicus: The navel or "belly button" that remains as a lifelong reminder of the fact that every human being was once nourished in a mother's uterus through the placenta.

Urethra: The short passage between the bladder and the outside of the body.

Uterine Neck: See *Cervix.*

Vagina: The passageway between the outside of a woman's body and the lower end of the uterus.

Vaginal Douche: Irrigation of the vagina with water or a medicinal solution.

Varicose Veins: Enlarged or dilated blood vessels.

Vernix Caseosa: The white creamy covering over the baby's skin during the last part of pregnancy. This is usually washed away before the father sees the child for the first time.

Version: An obstetric procedure whereby the doctor can turn the baby in the birth canal so that it will be in the most advantageous position for delivery.

Vulva: The most external parts of the vagina.

Zygote: The fertilized egg at any stage before cleavage, but is most narrowly restricted to the egg after the chromosome groups from ovum and sperm have come together.

Books to Read

ALDRICH, C. A. AND ALDRICH, M. M.: *Babies Are Human Beings.*
New York: Macmillan, 1939. This edition is practically a classic on
raising a young child, pointing out that even babies are human
and entitled to certain rights.

BING, E.: *Six Practical Lessons for an Easier Childbirth.* New York:
Grosset & Dunlap, 1967. The book contains an excellent description
of the exercises and techniques to prepare for labor by the Lamaze
method.

BING, E.: *The Adventure of Birth.* New York: Simon and Schuster,
Inc., 1970. Here is a collection of letters from parents who, having
used the Lamaze technique, describe their experiences in labor and
delivery.

CHABAN, I.: *Awake and Aware.* New York: Dell Books, 1966. An
informative book providing a general history of childbirth with
emphasis on the psychoprophylactic method (Lamaze technique).

DAY, B. AND LILEY, M. H.: *The Secret World of the Baby.* New York:
Random House, 1968. Just what title implies.

DICK-READ, G.: *Introduction to Motherhood.* New York: Harper &
Brothers, 1951. While written primarily for the woman, this book
will help you to understand some of the problems your wife will
face in labor and how she can prepare for them.

DICK-READ, G.: *Childbirth Without Fear.* New York: Harper &
Brothers, 1954. You can learn from the discussions how fear and
tension result in pain during labor and how to dispel these by
intelligent information.

EASTMAN, N. J. AND RUSSELL, K. P.: *Expectant Motherhood.* Boston:
Little, Brown and Company, 1970. Although primarily for your
wife, here is an authoritative book that you might find informative.

ELLIS, R. W. B.: *Child Health and Development.* New York: Grune
& Stratton, 1966. This edition (the fourth) deals with normal
development of the child and with those social agencies that have a
direct impact on the child.

ENGLISH, O. S. AND FOSTER, C. J.: *Fathers Are Parents Too!* New York: G. P. Putnam's Sons, 1951. The authors go into some detail on the importance of a good relationship between the father and his children and give some practical advice on how to establish this good relationship.

FLANAGAN, G. L.: *The First Nine Months of Life.* New York: Simon and Schuster, Inc., 1962. Told in a simple, non-technical narrative and illustrated by 132 photographs, this is an excellent account of the beginning of human life from the moment of conception to the hour of birth.

GELB, B.: *The ABC of Natural Childbirth.* New York: W. W. Norton & Company, Inc., 1954. Here is a mother's own story of her experience with natural childbirth in a large New York City maternity hospital.

GERSH, M. J.: *How to Raise Children at Home in Your Spare Time.* New York: Stein & Day, 1966. Written in an amusing style, here is help for the battered parent syndrome: how to make your first baby seem like your second.

GESELL, A. AND ILG, F. L.: *Infant and Child in the Culture of Today.* New York: Harper & Brothers, 1949. This is the first in the famous series of three volumes which tells parents what some children do at various stages of their growth and development, and not necessarily what you should expect your child to do.

GILBERT, M. S.: *Biography of the Unborn.* Baltimore, Md.: Williams & Wilkins Company, 1948. The narrative presents a rather detailed description of the development of the baby during the nine months of gestation.

GINOTT, H. G.: *Between Parent and Child.* New York: Macmillan, 1965. The information here is designed to help parents identify their goals in relation to children and suggest methods of achieving those goals.

GUTTMACHER, A. F.: *Pregnancy and Birth.* New York: The Viking Press, Inc., 1957. A thorough handbook, this edition covers the subjects mentioned in the title and goes into great detail on normal as well as abnormal aspects.

ILG, F. L. AND AMES, L. B.: *Child Behavior.* New York: Harper & Row, 1955. Here is a realistic guide to child behavior in the vital formative years from birth to ten.

ILLINGWORTH, R. S.: *The Normal Child.* Boston: Little, Brown & Co., 4th ed., 1968. The author includes chapters on the clumsy child, lying, stealing and overactivity.

KARMEL, M.: *Thank You, Dr. Lamaze*. Philadelphia: J. B. Lippincott Co., 1959. This is an excellent account of a woman's experiences in preparation for labor by the Lamaze method.

KENYON, J. H.: *Healthy Babies are Happy Babies*. Boston: Little, Brown & Co., 1940. The reliable information on the care, health, and feeding of children up to the age of three is worthy of review.

LA LECHE LEAGUE INTERNATIONAL: *The Womanly Art of Breast Feeding*. Franklin Park, Illinois, 1967. Here is a presentation of practical suggestions for breast feeding by women who are strongly committed to it.

LEVY, J. AND MUNROE, R.: *The Happy Family*. New York: Alfred A. Knopf, Inc., 1938. This deals with all aspects of the family and its problems.

MANN, D., WOODWORD, L. E., AND JOSEPH, N.: *Educating Expectant Parents*. New York: Visiting Nurse Service of New York, 1961. The authors share their observations and recommendations for education and training of visiting nurses in the teaching and guidance of young parents with particular reference to the emotional and mental health of children.

MILLER, W.: *This World Is Young*. New York: Simon and Schuster, 1958. This photographic exploration of the world of childhood is fascinating.

NEW YORK CITY DEPARTMENT OF HEALTH: *Baby Book*. 1970. A handbook for parents, this book covers most of the questions and problems that arise during the first two years of a baby's life.

POPENOE, P.: *Marriage—Before and After*. New York: Wilfred Funk, Inc., 1943. Although the book discusses marriage in general, it does give specific information about the role of the child in the relationship.

RIBBLE, M. A.: *The Rights of Infants*. New York: Columbia University Press, 1943. A scholarly work on modern concepts of child rearing. Nevertheless, this edition contains a good deal of material suitable for the general reader.

RUGH, R. AND SHETTLES, L.: *From Conception to Birth*. New York: Harper & Row, 1971. Excellent color photographs.

SCHEINFELD, A.: *Your Heredity and Environment*. New York: J. B. Lippincott, 1965. An excellent discussion of what you can expect your baby to be like.

SENN, M. J. AND SOLNIT, A. J.: *Problems in Child Behavior and Development*. Philadelphia, Pa.: Lea & Febiger, 1968. Here is a description of the philosophy and methods at Yale Child Study Center of dealing with parents and children in distress.

SPOCK, B.: *Baby and Child Care.* New York: Pocket Books, 1968. This is the classic reference on medical and psychological aspects of raising the young child.

THOMS, H., ROTH, L. G., AND LINTON, D.: *Understanding Natural Childbirth.* New York: McGraw-Hill, Inc., 1950. This contains a well-illustrated and simply-worded explanation of what to expect in labor.

UNITED STATES DEPARTMENT OF HEALTH, EDUCATION AND WELFARE: *Infant Care.* Washington, D.C.: U. S. Government Printing Office, 1969. An excellent and inexpensive pamphlet. Others in the series, equally good, are: *Your Child from One to Six, The Child from Six to Twelve, Guiding the Adolescent* and *A Healthy Personality for Your Child.*

Index

163